ELI • 228

Armies of Russia's War in Ukraine

MARK GALEOTTI

ILLUSTRATED BY ADAM HOOK
Series editor Martin Windrow

OSPREY PUBLISHING
Bloomsbury Publishing Plc

Kemp House, Chawley Park, Cumnor Hill, Oxford OX2 9PH, UK
29 Earlsfort Terrace, Dublin 2, Ireland
1385 Broadway, 5th Floor, New York, NY 10018, USA
Email: info@ospreypublishing.com
www.ospreypublishing.com

OSPREY is a trademark of Osprey Publishing Ltd

First published in Great Britain in 2019

© Osprey Publishing Ltd, 2019

Transferred to digital print in 2023

A catalogue record for this book is available from the British Library.

Print ISBN: PB 978 1 4728 3344 0
eBook: 978 1 4728 3345 7
ePDF: 978 1 4728 3346 4
XML: 978 1 4728 3343 3

Editor: Martin Windrow
Maps by www.bounford.com
Index by Alan Rutter
Typeset by PDQ Digital Media Solutions, Bungay, UK
Printed and bound in Great Britain by CPI (Group) UK Ltd, Croydon CR0 4YY

23 24 25 26 27   10 9 8 7 6 5

The Woodland Trust
Osprey Publishing supports the Woodland Trust, the UK's leading woodland
conservation charity.

www.ospreypublishing.com
To find out more about our authors and books visit our website. Here you will
find extracts, author interviews, details of forthcoming events and the option
to sign-up for our newsletter.

AUTHOR'S NOTE

Translating out of Cyrillic always poses challenges, and especially here;
Russian and Ukrainian, while close, are nonetheless different languages,
and language has become a politically sensitive issue. I have chosen to
transliterate well-known names as they are pronounced (so the letter ë
becomes yo), and have ignored the diacritical signs found in the original.
Ukrainian words, names and places are transliterated Ukrainian-style, while
Russian ones are rendered in their form. Thus, although Russian-speaking
insurgents would refer to e.g. Donbass, Lugansk and Slavyansk, these are
rendered as Donbas, Luhansk and Slovyansk. References to Kiev rather than
Kyiv relate to the period before 1991, when the Russian form of the
Ukrainian capital was most widely used. For names, the individuals'
preferred forms are used, so the rebel Khodakovsky is Alexander, while the
Ukrainian politician Turchinov is Olexander.
Likewise, the term to use for local and transplanted fighters in the Donbas
is a vexed question. On the one hand, it is clear that Moscow stirred up,
arms, supports and generally controls them; on the other, this is not purely
a Russian initiative, since many locals with strong grievances chose to turn
against Kyiv. For the sake of brevity, the terms "rebel," "insurgent," and
"militia" are all used for proxy forces not directly made up of regular Russian
troops, but with the understanding that this inevitably simplifies a complex
reality.

ARTIST'S NOTE

Readers may care to note that the original paintings from which the color
plates in this book were prepared are available for private sale. All
reproduction copyright whatsoever is retained by the publisher. All
inquiries should be addressed to:

Scorpio, 158 Mill Road, Hailsham, East Sussex, BN27 2SH, UK
scorpiopaintings@btinternet.com

The publishers regret that they can enter into no correspondence upon
this matter.

Abbreviations used in this text

ATO	Anti-Terrorist Operation
DNR	Donetsk People's Republic
FSB	Federal Security Service (Russian domestic security service)
GRU	Main Intelligence Directorate (Russian military intelligence)
KSO	Special Operations Command (Russian)
LNR	Luhansk People's Republic
MGB	Ministry of State Security (DNR/LNR)
MVD	Ministry of Internal Affairs (DNR/LNR)
MVS	Ministry of Internal Affairs (Ukraine)
RGSO	Republic State Guard Service (DNR)
SBU	Ukrainian Security Service

Order of battle abbreviations

A. Aslt	air assault
A. Av	Army Aviation
Abn	airborne
AD	air defense
Ambl	airmobile
Armd	armored
Art	artillery
AT	antitank
Bde	brigade
Bn	battalion
Bty	battery
BTG	battalion tactical group
Comms	communications/signals
Co	company
Div	division
Indep	independent
Inf	infantry
Mech	mechanized
MLRS	multiple-launch rocket system
Mot	motorized
MR	motor rifle (motorized infantry)
Mtn	mountain
NI	Naval Infantry
NG	National Guard
RA	rocket artillery
Recon	reconnaissance
Regt	regiment
SP	self-propelled
Spec Des	Special Designation (*Spetsnaz*)
TDB	Territorial Defense Battalion

CONTENTS

ARMIES OF RUSSIA'S WAR IN UKRAINE

INTRODUCTION

When Russian forces, fully armed yet stripped of their insignia, fanned out across the Crimean Peninsula in March 2014, they were not just seizing territory that Moscow considered historically its own: they were also opening a new chapter in a complex relationship rooted in kinship and difference, shared history and divergent politics.

The very name Ukraine springs from the word for "border," yet it can rightly call itself the heart and wellspring of the Rus people. Its capital, Kiev, was politically and culturally dominant amongst their city-states before it was sacked by the invading Mongols in 1240. During the years of Mongol domination, the small town of Moscow and the ruthlessly opportunistic Rurikid dynasty that controlled it rose to assume Kiev's place. Ukraine would be contested between Orthodox Muscovy and the Catholic Poles and Lithuanians until falling under the rule of Russia in 1654. Ukraine, part Orthodox and part Catholic, would essentially remain part of the Russian Empire for the next three and a half centuries, despite periodic risings and atrocities, such as the *Holodomor*, the enforced mass starvation whereby Soviet dictator Joseph Stalin broke Ukrainian resistance to his rule in the 1930s. During World War II Ukrainians fought both for and against the USSR and the German occupiers, and the last anti-Soviet guerrillas were not crushed until the mid-1950s.

Nationalism was rekindled in Ukraine in the 1980s, as the Soviet Union ground towards its end. On August 24, 1991 the country formally declared itself independent, although achieving this in practice would take months of disengagement. Nonetheless, a referendum ratified this decision, with more than 90 percent of voters backing independence. The Soviet Union itself was formally dissolved at the end of 1991.

In common with many other post-Soviet states suddenly thrust into statehood, Ukraine suffered from serious economic, social and political challenges. Inflation skyrocketed and the economy shrank. Despite several dramatic expressions of popular dissatisfaction

A *Berkut* riot policeman (left) with a bloodied protester during the February 2014 demonstrations in Kyiv. Note his riot armor, the eagle patch on his sleeve, and the distinctive blue-and-gray tiger-stripe camouflage uniform – see Plate A2. (Mstyslav Chernov/Wikimedia Commons/CC-BY-SA 3.0)

with corrupt governments and their empty promises – notably the 2004–05 "Orange Revolution" following rigged elections – Ukraine remained torn between its hopes of building a liberal, economically vibrant, European democracy, and a reality characterized by systemic corruption, inefficiency and economic decay.

In 2013, President Viktor Yanukovych made a momentous political mistake when he flip-flopped on a proposed treaty with the European Union. Like so many of the so-called "Donetsk mafia" politicians from the east of the country, Yanukovych looked to Putin's ascendant Russia for patronage and profit. Moscow was determined that Ukraine would remain within its sphere of influence, but national sentiment, particularly in the west of the country, wanted closer ties to the European Union. Having initially backed an Association Agreement with the EU in 2013, Yanukovych then reversed his policy once Moscow made its hostility clear.

Protests began in Kyiv's main Independence Square, and initial attempts to disperse them only galvanized the opposition and brought more to join the rising. The government tried several times to use force to end the so-called "Euromaidan" demonstrations, but with a mix of brutality and inconsistency that only worsened the situation. On February 22, 2014, facing the threat of impeachment and with his government collapsing around him, Yanukovych fled to Russia, leaving behind 130 dead and a country rethinking its place in the world. Moscow, alarmed at the prospect of a new Ukrainian government committed to breaking free of its influence, began making its own plans.

TAKING CRIMEA

The situation was especially complex in Crimea, the peninsula on the country's southern coast, which was also still home to Russia's Black Sea Fleet. It had been part of the Russian Socialist Federal Soviet Republic until 1954, when Soviet leader Nikita Khrushchev (himself a Ukrainian) transferred it to Ukraine. Nonetheless, much of its population was culturally Russian. In 1990 almost all Ukrainians voted for independence from the USSR, but this prospect received a much more lukewarm 56 percent endorsement in Crimea, and since then Crimeans had often felt neglected by Kyiv.

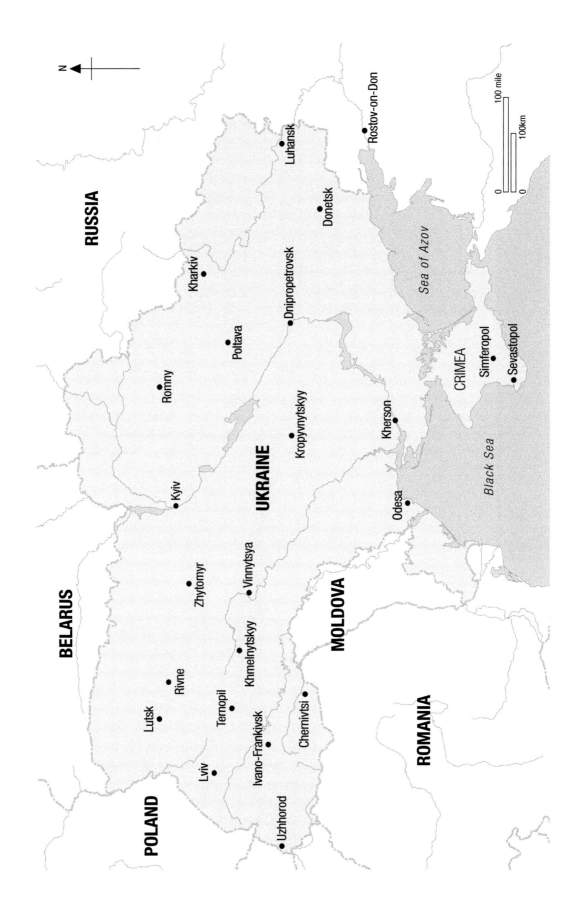

Russian Defense Minister Sergei Shoigu (left) confers with his Chief of the General Staff, Gen Valery Gerasimov; these were the military architects of President Putin's seizure of Crimea and the subsequent operation in the Donbas. (Kremlin.ru/CC-BY-SA 4.0)

The Kremlin was alarmed that the collapse of the Yanukovych regime and the emergence of a new government avowedly committed to closer relations with the West – maybe even joining NATO – put its strategic positions in Crimea at risk. Its 1997 agreement with Kyiv on basing the Black Sea Fleet and up to 25,000 military personnel on the peninsula ran through to 2042, but even so there were many in Moscow who were unwilling to put their faith in what they saw as an illegitimate and nationalistic new regime. Besides this, President Vladimir Putin of Russia, who had enjoyed sky-high approval ratings for so much of his time in office, was now watching these figures fall. He knew full well that most Russians believed that Crimea was really part of their own country, unfairly handed to Ukraine. With Putin also apparently coming more and more to believe his own mythology and looking to establish his place in history as the man who "made Russia great again," political, military and strategic interests all seemed to converge.

The decision-making about Crimea took place behind the scenes and largely involved only a handful of Putin's closest (and typically most hawkish) confidants. On February 20, 2014, two days before Yanukovych fled the country, the decision appears to have been made to take the peninsula. *Vremya cha* – zero hour – was set for February 27, 2014.

More than a tenth of Ukraine's military strength, some 22,000 military personnel, were based in Crimea. Most, however, were naval personnel, and none were kept at a particularly high state of readiness. Beyond naval and coastal defense missile forces, as well as an Air Force brigade and three antiaircraft missile regiments, there were only a single regular Army battalion and several Naval Infantry (marine) units. While the latter were relatively well trained, they were all suffering from the disruption and demoralization caused by years of under-funding. Beyond that, there were three brigades and two battalions of paramilitary Interior Troops, subordinated to the Ministry of Internal Security (MVS), and a Border Guard battalion which, while primarily intended for police and security missions, had a secondary

BMD-2 light airmobile personnel carriers of a Russian paratroop unit being offloaded in Sevastopol from the Ropucha-class large landing ship *Tsesar Kunikov*. The Russians' capacity to rapidly reinforce their expeditionary force in Crimea was crucial to consolidating their seizure of the peninsula. (Ministry of Defense of the Russian Federation/Mil.ru/CC-BY-SA 4.0)

national defense role. The crucial issue, however, once the Russians made their move, would be the lack of clear orders and, according to some, willful confusion in the chain of command by officers hostile to the new regime.

Already, Russia's forces on the peninsula included parts of two Naval Infantry brigades, and in the days leading up to the operation they were brought up to combat readiness, with some elements being sent out from their bases to secure airfields and arms depots. Meanwhile, Special Forces across the country were quietly activated under the cover of "snap inspections," many being airlifted to the Russian airbase at Anapa and naval base at Novorossisk, both on the Black Sea and close to Crimea. Officers of the

A

UKRAINIAN ARMY & POLICE, 2009–14

(1) Ukrainian general officer, 2013

The Soviet legacy of Ukrainian uniforms, especially before 2014, is especially clear in parade dress. The Chief of the Ukrainian General Staff, ColGen Volodymyr Zamana, is shown here taking the salute in a uniform that differs from his Soviet forebears and Russian counterparts only in the patches on the sleeves and the national emblem pin on his breast. The broad, high-crowned peaked cap is particularly characteristic, as is the "wave-green" color; note the three stars of colonel-general's rank on his shoulder straps.

(2) *Berkut* riot policeman, 2014

The pivot of modern Ukrainian history was the Maidan rising of 2013–14, when protestors filled the square of that name in Kyiv. They faced often-violent clashes with supporters of President Yanukovych's government and, far more often, with police. Members of the infamous *Berkut* ("Golden Eagle") riot police were at the heart of attempts to disperse the protestors, and sometimes used lethal force. This officer is wearing riot armor over his distinctive "tiger-stripe" uniform in dark blue, blue-gray and gray, with the *Berkut* patch on his right sleeve and its name on a chest tab almost hidden by his armor. His weapon is a Fort-500M pump-action shotgun, specially designed by the Ukrainian Interior Ministry's own research center; it can fire non-lethal rounds, but in this case is loaded with solid slugs.

(3) UKRPOLBAT soldier; Kosovo, 2009

As an early sign of willingness to cooperate with its Western neighbors, in 1998 Kyiv agreed (despite considerable domestic opposition) to form the Ukrainian-Polish Peace Force Battalion (UKRPOLBAT or POLUKRBAT) for international peace-keeping and humanitarian operations. In 2000 this unit was deployed to Kosovo as part of the UN's KFOR mission, and this paratrooper is manning a checkpoint outside Raka in southern Kosovo in 2009. He has a non-standard but widely used load-bearing vest over his forest-camouflage uniform, under which he sports the blue-and-white striped *telnyashka* inherited from Soviet paratroopers; note the blue-and-yellow Ukrainian flag patch on his sleeve pocket. His AK-74 rifle is, unusually, the full-stocked version instead of the folding-stock AKS-74. The signboard bears the shield badges of KFOR (subdued shades) and POLUKRBAT (full color); the lettering in white capitals reads "KFOR/ BORDER CROSING [*sic*] POINT/ BY PASS."

(4) Ukrainian Ministry of Defense badge & patch

These show the *tryzub* trident, the traditional symbol of Ukrainian sovereignty dating back to the 10th-century Prince Volodymyr the Great. The shield is set against a ceremonial mace, above crossed swords and a scroll, and supported by figures of a crowned lion rampant and a rifleman in traditional costume.

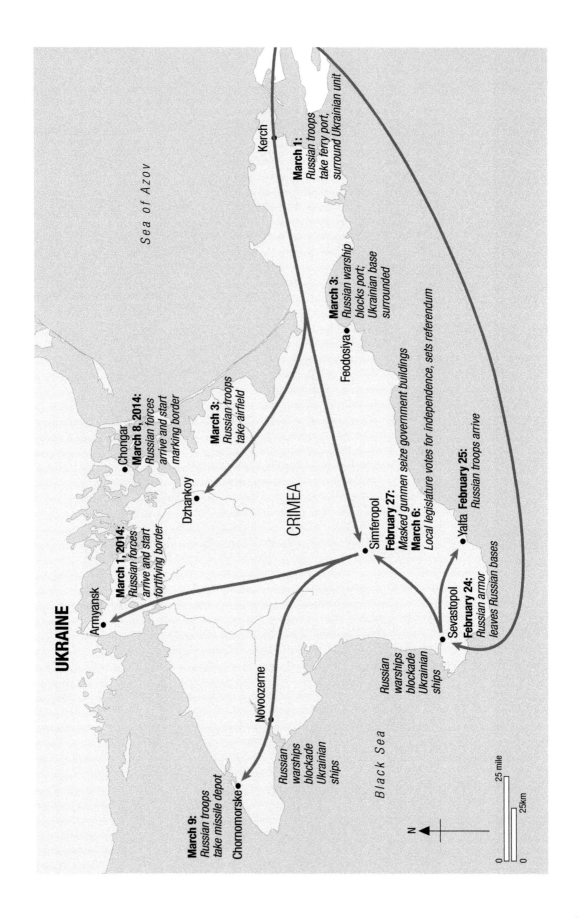

UKRAINE

March 1, 2014:
Russian forces arrive and start fortifying border
Armyansk

March 8, 2014:
Russian forces arrive and start marking border
Chongar

March 3:
Russian troops take airfield
Dzhankoy

CRIMEA

Simferopol
February 27:
Masked gunmen seize government buildings
March 6:
Local legislature votes for independence, sets referendum

March 9:
Russian troops take missile depot
Chornomorske

Novoozerne

Russian warships blockade Ukrainian ships

March 1:
Russian troops take ferry port, surround Ukrainian unit
Kerch

March 3:
Russian warship blocks port; Ukrainian base surrounded
Feodosiya

Yalta
February 25:
Russian troops arrive

Sevastopol
February 24:
Russian armor leaves Russian bases

Russian warships blockade Ukrainian ships

Sea of Azov

Black Sea

N

25 mile
25km
0
0

10

Table 1: Ukrainian ground forces in Crimea, March 2014

Armed forces:
36th Indep Mech Coastal Defense Bde (at Perevalnoye)
1st Indep Naval Inf Bn (Feodosiya)
501st Indep Naval Inf Bn (Kerch)
56th Indep Guards Bn (Sevastopol)
406th Indep Artillery Bde (Simferopol)
37th Indep Comms and Control Rgt (Sevastopol)

Interior troops:
9th Indep Interior Troops Bde (Simferopol)
42nd Indep Interior Troops Bde (Sevastopol)
47th Indep Interior Troops Bde (Feodosia)
15th Indep Interior Troops Bn (Yevpatoria)
18th Mot Police Bn (Gaspra)

Border guards:
Indep Special Purpose Border Guard Bn (Yalta)

GRU military intelligence service and Federal Security Service (FSB) began brokering deals with local sympathizers, including organized crime groups, to ensure that when the operation began there would be well-armed "local self-defense groups" on the streets.

At around 4.30am on February 27 men wearing a motley array of camouflage uniforms, but carrying a suspiciously modern and extensive range of weapons, seized the local parliament building in Simferopol and hoisted the Russian flag. Calling themselves "Crimea's armed self-defense force," they were actually operators from KSO, Russia's newly formed Special Operations Command, supported by *Spetsnaz* commandos from other detachments, and by Naval Infantry.[1] There were also other "volunteers"; these would often prove to be little more than thuggish looters, with the exception of a few units such as former *Berkut* riot police who had joined the anti-Kyiv side, or "Rubezh," a unit of veterans. These "deniable" groups gave the Russians political cover as their own well-trained and well-armed forces, uniforms bare of any insignia, fanned out to seize the peninsula.

Over the course of the next few days and weeks (see map) the Russians blockaded the Ukrainian forces in Crimea, closed the neck of the peninsula to reinforcements, and set up a puppet government. Their claim that the soldiers were not Russian – Vladimir Putin memorably suggested that they could have bought their latest-issue *Ratnik*-model uniforms and equipment at second-hand shops – sufficed to introduce a note of uncertainty into the situation. That, combined with the speed and professionalism of the operation, and the chaos on the government side (Kyiv did not even have a minister of defense until the afternoon of the 27th) helps explain why, at first, a relative handful of Russian Special Forces (probably no more than 2,000 in the first few days), along with local allies of often dubious effectiveness, managed to bottle up much larger Ukrainian forces. Over time, however, the Russians would send heavier equipment to Crimea, including artillery, air defense, and mechanized units, as well as Mi-35M helicopter gunships.

A Russian Naval *Spetsnaz* soldier, photographed outside Perevalne base in Crimea (note the Ukrainian naval symbolism on the wall) before it surrendered. As well as his AK-74 he holds an R-168-0,5U radio – compare with Plate B1. (Anton Holoborodko/ Wikimedia Commons/CC-BY-SA 3.0)

1 See Elite 206, *Spetsnaz: Russia's Special Forces*

Table 2: Russian ground forces in Crimea operation, February–March 2014

Based in Crimea, elements of:
510th Naval Inf Bde (Feodosiya)
810th Indep Naval Inf Bde (Simferopol)

Deployed to Crimea, elements of:
7th Guards Air Assault Div (Novorossisk)
3rd Indep Special Designation Bde (Tolyatti)
10th Indep Spec Des Bde (Krasnodar)
16th Indep Spec Des Bde (Tambov)
18th Guards Indep MR Bde (Grozny)
22nd Indep Spec Des Bde (Stepnoi)
31st Guards Indep Air Assault Bde (Ulyanovsk)
291st Artillery Bde (Troitskaya)
25th Indep Spec Des Regt (Stavropol)
45th Indep Spec Des Air Assault Regt (Kubinka, Moscow)
382nd Indep Naval Inf Bn (Temryuk)
727th Indep Naval Inf Bn (Astrakhan)
Special Operations Command (Prokhladny)

One by one, the Ukrainian units either fled (many Coast Guard ships managed to avoid capture), surrendered, or defected. In a particular blow, the highest-ranking Ukrainian officer in Crimea, Rear Admiral Denis Berezovsky, defected and was made deputy commander of the Russian Black Sea Fleet. On March 16, Moscow held a carefully managed referendum in Crimea, which duly produced a 97 percent vote in favor of joining Russia, and over the course of the next month the last Ukrainian loyalist forces were allowed to leave. The seizure of the Crimea resulted in only two casualties: a Ukrainian Navy warrant officer, and a Russian "volunteer."

WAR IN THE DONBAS

In June 2014, when it was already clear that Moscow's follow-on operation in southeastern Ukraine was not going to plan, a former Russian General Staff officer told the author that "had the Ukrainians fought for Crimea, we would not now be fighting in the Donbas." The ease of the peninsula's seizure and the disarray in Kyiv encouraged Putin and his advisers to make a fateful

The spark that ignited the war in the Donbas: "Strelkov's" fighters seize control of government buildings in Slovyansk on April 12, 2014. All wear the same Spectre-S Skvo camouflage, and carry AK-74s and RPG-26 rocket launchers. (Yevgen Nasadyuk/Wikimedia Commons/CC-BY-SA 3.0)

Slovyansk

Severodonetsk

Kramatorsk

UKRAINE

Artemivsk

Pervomaisk

Luhansk

Zaitseve

Alchevsk

Debaltseve

LUHANSK PEOPLE'S REPUBLIC

Horlivka

Avdiivka

Krasny Luch

○
**MH17
crash**

Antratsit

Donetsk

Zellenopillya

Ilovaisk

DONETSK PEOPLE'S REPUBLIC

RUSSIA

Mariupol

Novoazovsk

Rostov-on-Dor

Sea of Azov

N

····· line of contact

0   25 mile

0   25km

over-reach. Crimea, after all, had been a unique case: a peninsula where Russia already had a military presence, whose population in the main felt unhappy with how Kyiv had treated them for years, and which the majority of Russians justifiably felt was theirs. Nonetheless, although not part of the original plan, after seizing Crimea the Kremlin began contemplating a limited and deniable military operation in the ethnically Russian east of Ukraine. The aim this time was not territorial conquest, but political control: to convince Kyiv that Moscow could and would punish it for any moves towards closer integration with the West. The Kremlin assumed that this limited adventure would intimidate Ukraine, and force it to accept that it was part of Russia's sphere of influence. This was a serious miscalculation.

There were genuine grievances and concerns in Eastern Ukraine, which had been Yanukovych's power base and was also disproportionately populated by Russian-speakers. These had understandable concerns about the implications of the new government in Kyiv, but what they wanted was not so much independence as greater autonomy. These worries were at once magnified by Moscow's media, which began characterizing the new government as a "fascist junta," while efforts were made to stir protests into violent risings. In many of the cities in the east these efforts failed, either because of a lack of real support or due to the timely and effective work of Kyiv's security forces. In the cities of Donetsk and Luhansk, however, protesters stormed local government buildings and called for referenda on self-determination. Acting Ukrainian president Olexander Turchinov angrily threatened "counter-terrorism measures"; all that was needed now was a spark.

That spark was provided by 52 volunteers and mercenaries from Crimea commanded by an ardent Russian nationalist (and former intelligence officer) named Igor Girkin, although better known as Igor Strelkov after his call sign *Strelok*, meaning "shooter" or "gunman." On April 12, 2014 he led his force

B

CRIMEA, FEBRUARY 2014

(1) Lieutenant, Russian *Spetsnaz*
This officer of Naval *Spetsnaz* oversees the removal of Ukrainian marines from their base at Feodosiya. Like all the so-called "little green men," he displays no insignia, but – in a practice not seen elsewhere during the operation – he has two lines chalked on the side of his ShBM composite helmet, informally denoting his rank, and for this reason the helmet has no camouflage cover. Otherwise he is wearing the most recent *Ratnik* battledress, including a 6B33 armor vest and 6Sh117 tactical vest; he is reporting on his 168-0.5UME tactical radio, while covering the Ukrainians with his AKM-74 rifle accessorized with a 1P87 collimator sight (an optical sight with an illuminated aiming-point), and a GP-34 grenade launcher.

(2) Marine, Ukrainian 1st Independent Naval Infantry Battalion
This dejected marine, carrying his personal effects in a plastic laundry bag, is leaving his base after a negotiated surrender which allowed those soldiers who were willing to change sides to leave with their possessions but not their weapons. His black Naval Infantry beret bears the other-ranks' badge featuring a winged sword on an anchor; the officers' version is larger, incorporating oakleaves. He wears the traditional striped vest under camouflaged winter battledress with a thin black "fleece" collar lining. Note the subdued patches on his left sleeve: a Ukrainian sword/trident motif, above the wolf-head unit symbol set against a flag, a black cross and crossed swords (compare with B4 below).

(3) Crimean "Self-Defense Auxiliary"
To maintain the fiction that Crimea was rising against Kyiv rather than being invaded, Moscow supplemented its forces with local militias and mercenaries. Some were sympathetic local police, others – as in this case – local criminals pressed into service in return for favors. This man wears a private purchase winter jacket in VSR-98 Flora camouflage, with an orange-and-black St George's ribbon added as a loyalist field sign. His new AKS-74U carbine was probably part of the price exacted by his gang for supporting the invasion. He appears to be a spotter, judging by the vintage Soviet BPV 7x50 binoculars, though the evidence of beer consumption calls into question how useful an asset he would actually be.

(4) Ukrainian 501st Naval Infantry Battalion sleeve patch
This unit was based at Kerch in the northeast of Crimea. Part of 36th Bde, it was forced to surrender to Russian special forces. Some of its men chose to defect, but most were repatriated; the unit is now headquartered at Mariupol, where it continues to take part in fighting along the line of contact. The design of the patch is common to all such units, apart from a distinguishing central motif: here the 501st's griffin, and in B2 the 1st Bn's right-facing yellow wolf-head. The scrolls read "NAVAL/ INFANTRY."

The shooting-down of MH17

On July 17, 2014, Malaysia Airlines Flight 17 (MH17) was on a scheduled run from Amsterdam to Kuala Lumpur. While flying over Eastern Ukraine the Boeing 777-200ER was hit by a missile and crashed, killing all 283 passengers and 15 crew on board. Although Moscow has advanced numerous alternative explanations, the Dutch-led Joint Investigation Team concluded that it was shot down by a Buk M1 SA-11 surface-to-air missile fired from separatist-controlled territory in Ukraine. The system in question appears to have been one of several originally fielded by Russia's 53rd Anti-Aircraft Rocket Bde, supplied to the rebels probably complete with crew. Judging by a subsequently deleted social media post from Strelkov, the rebels thought the target was a Ukrainian An-26 transport plane. The presence of heavy weapons systems such as the SA-11 demonstrate how quickly Moscow moved to support the rebels, and the provision of AA missiles in particular helps explain why Ukraine has not been able to make much use of its air assets. However, there is no evidence that Russian military commanders were involved in the launch decision – which underlines the relative autonomy of their proxy warlords at that time.

A Russian Buk M1-2 SA-II SAM system, with 9A310M1-2 missiles, photographed at the Moscow Air Show in 2005. (Public Domain/.: Ajvol:.)

to seize local police and government buildings in the town of Slovyansk. An initial response by operators from the SBU, Ukraine's Security Service, was driven off, and Kyiv began mustering more formidable forces. Meanwhile, as

From a firing position in the ruins of the much fought-over Donetsk Airport in the Donbas, a rebel soldier mans a 12.7mm NSV heavy machine gun. (Mstyslav Chernov/Wikimedia Commons/CC-BY-SA 4.0)

Men self-identifying as Cossacks feature prominently among the volunteers on both sides. Here a member of the DNR police, wearing the distinctive Cossack hat, inspects a rocket that landed outside his checkpoint near Donetsk; typically, lack of a military radio obliges him to pass his report by cellphone. All three men wear a mixture of camouflage uniform and Gorka-4 mountain suits. (Photo by Pierre Crom/ Getty Images)

the rebels in Slovyansk managed to hold off successive government assaults, the rebellion spread.

The initial fighting involved not just Ukrainian government forces but also pro-government militias backed by a range of interests, from political movements to powerful businessmen. Arrayed against them was an equally varied mix of separatist militias, some made up of locals, others of mercenaries and volunteers from Russia – often with encouragement, weapons and guidance from Moscow. This was a messy, dirty conflict from the first, with both sides being credibly accused of human-rights abuses. While cities such as Mariupol and Svyatokhirsk were recaptured by the government, the tide seemed to be flowing against them.

In May, the leaders of the self-proclaimed Donetsk People's Republic (DNR) and Luhansk People's Republic (LNR) announced their independence from Ukraine, and that they were forming a confederation known as *Novorossiya* – "New Russia" – with Strelkov as their defense minister. This project came to nothing, however; Strelkov was dismissed in August, and the dream of Novorossiya was dead by the end of the year.

Instead, 2014 saw Russia increasingly mixing its own soldiers and even whole units in with the insurgent militias, especially to provide higher-order firepower and more disciplined forces. This was not enough, however, and as government forces began pushing into rebel-held areas, retaking Slovyansk and encircling Donetsk, Moscow was forced to escalate, sending more of its own troops into the field. The period of a so-called "hybrid war," one in which disinformation, deniable political operations, and other "non-kinetic" means were at least as important as the actual fighting on the battlefield, was virtually over. Instead this was looking much more like a conventional (even if undeclared) war, in which both sides fielded mixes of regular forces and militias in sporadic but brutal conflict.

The battalion tactical groups committed by Russia were able to break the Ukrainian advance, inflicting a shattering defeat at Ilovaisk. This would set a new pattern; where they could, the Russians would rely on their proxy militias, but despite efforts to build them into a serious conventional army they were often undisciplined (witness the tragic shooting-down of the MH17 airliner in July 2014), or simply outgunned. Whenever Ukrainian government forces looked as if they were likely to make serious gains, the Russians would surge in their own troops to turn the tide.

Meanwhile, the insurgents were able to use this opportunity to make local gains of their own. For example, after a lengthy and brutal battle which at its worst was reminiscent of the street-fighting in Stalingrad, Donetsk airport fell to insurgents in January 2015. This was despite the astonishing tenacity of the mixed government and militia forces defending it, earning them the nickname "cyborgs" for their apparent tirelessness and indestructability. In February 2015, rebels also finally took the contested town of Debaltseve, eliminating a salient of government-held territory that otherwise cut between Donetsk and Luhansk.

The front lines would ebb and flow, and towns such as Debaltseve would change hands several times. However, in broad terms, by mid-2015 the state of the conflict was set. To newly elected Ukrainian President Petro Poroshenko's government, this was an "Anti-Terrorist Operation" (ATO). To the Kremlin, it was not a war at all; only in December 2015 did Putin finally admit that there were Russians in the Donbas "resolving various issues," but even then he denied that they were combat forces. Both the September 2014 Minsk Protocol, negotiated under the auspices of the Organization for Security and Cooperation in Europe, and the February 2015 Minsk II agreement, agreed by Ukraine, Russia, France and Germany, have failed to bring any lasting peace. Instead, the pattern has been one of on-off ceasefires, sporadic local fighting, mutual shelling, and equally mutual recrimination.

Through 2015 and 2016 there was much fighting, but little real change; indeed, 2016 was the first year in which the government, now deploying increasingly competent and confident forces, lost no ground to the rebels, and was able to concentrate on modernizing its forces and fortifying the front line. However, January 2017 saw a battle for the government-held town of Avdiivka that was reminiscent of the full-on warfare of 2014, with massed artillery bombardments and close ground engagements. The

A rebel fighter with an SVD sniper rifle passes the burnt-out remains of a Ukrainian government MT-LB after the recapture of Vuglerirsk (Uglegorsk) in 2015. (Photo by Pierre Crom/Getty Images)

government forces managed to hold the line, and in 2018 Kyiv adopted a new vocabulary: the rebel areas were "temporarily occupied territories," and the ATO was now a "Joint Forces Operation."

What may seem like an essentially meaningless bit of wordplay does have significance, as it also coincides with a more assertive line from the government forces. By 2017 they were episodically nudging their positions forward, deeper into the so-called "gray zone," the no-man's land along the line of contact. Ostensibly intended to secure more defensible positions with better observation opportunities, these also represent a creeping challenge to the current front line, and as of the time of writing in late 2018 it remains to be seen if and when this triggers some serious response from the Russians – who seem to have come to understand that they are stuck in a quagmire.

A Ukrainian government soldier in a particularly exposed position, firing a DShKM 12.7mm (.50cal) heavy machine gun. This modernized version of a design dating back to 1946 is still a brutally powerful weapon, if often inaccurate. (Public Domain/Staff Sgt Adriana M. Diaz-Brown)

Rather than inducing Kyiv to capitulate, their intervention into the Donbas has generated an unprecedented sense of Ukrainian national identity, and has helped galvanize serious military reform at last. Meanwhile, Moscow is having to subsidize the unrecognized pseudo-states of the Donbas as well as defending them. Unwilling to acknowledge failure, and so far unlikely to face a military defeat, Russia's forces – and the proxy armies they have raised, equipped and supported – remain in the disputed region.

So too does the human tragedy of the war. As of 2018, its toll has been estimated at more than 10,000 dead, and nearly two million internally displaced. The urbanized and industrialized Donbas region once held nearly 15 percent of Ukraine's population and generated an equal share of its gross domestic product (GDP), but now the economies of the DNR and LNR are in an appalling state, and Moscow is covertly having to subsidize them. According to Ukraine's National Security and Defense Council, this is costing it $3 billion a year, at least as much as all military operations. Even those parts of the region not controlled by the rebels are suffering from economic dislocation and the presence of populations of refugees. Kyiv may have been able to leverage its status as a victim of Russian aggression to win itself more support and tolerance in the West than might otherwise have been the case, but nonetheless it has also had to devote 5 percent of its GDP to national defense.

THE REBELS

The bulk of anti-government forces in the Donbas are proxies: local militias (in some cases, essentially organized criminal gangs given official status), volunteers, defectors from government forces, Cossacks, and mercenaries.[2] Some formed in early 2014 out of genuine hostility to the new government in Kyiv, but many were also created by Russian FSB or GRU operatives,

---

2 Historically frontier peoples enjoying a particular relationship with the Tsarist government, today's "Cossacks" are essentially a re-invented community, based on people who claim descent from the old Cossack culture that was virtually wiped out by Stalin. They are largely found in southern Russia and southeastern Ukraine; many of them support the traditional Russian Orthodox Church and muscular Russian nationalism.

"Igor Strelkov"

The man who by his own account started the Donbas war is generally known as "Strelkov" after his call sign *Strelok* (meaning "shooter" or "gunman"), who was made "defense minister" of the self-proclaimed DNR at the end of April 2014.

This ardently outspoken Russian nationalist is actually Igor Vsevolodovich Girkin, a former artillery officer (and, incidentally, a keen military re-enactor). With a background in the Russian security services – he says the FSB, although others have claimed he was in the GRU – he was involved in organizing "self-defense volunteers" for the Crimea operation. He has also been linked with a variety of often dirty civil wars over two decades: supporting pro-Moscow separatists in Moldova in 1992, Serbs in the 1992–95 Bosnian War, and fighting against rebels in Chechnya in 1999–2005. In many of these conflicts he was subsequently accused of human-rights abuses.

He appears to have been a ruthless and competent commander, but his uncompromising views and his apparent involvement in the shooting-down of MH17 made him both an embarrassment and a political threat. He became increasingly critical of Moscow as it backed away from supporting the *Novorossiya* project and outright annexation, and in August 2014 he was dismissed from his position under Kremlin pressure. He returned to Russia, where he continued to be a vocal critic of Putin's government as inconsistent and weak in its defense of Russian interests and nationals abroad.

Copying the Coalition in Iraq, the Ukrainian government produced a set of playing cards with the names and faces of rebel leaders to help troops identify them in case of capture. The top card shown here has the distinctive features of "Strelkov" – see Plate C3. (Viktoria Pryshutova/Wikimedia Commons/CC-BY-SA 3.0)

and even those which emerged independently have been brought under the control of the Russian-dominated DNR and LNR "People's Militias." This is the price the anti-Kyiv insurgents pay for money, weapons, ammunition, and equipment. The mysterious assassinations of several of their more willful commanders, blamed on Ukraine yet bearing all the signs of "inside jobs," have also shown what happens to those who fail to heed their paymasters.

Strelkov had nurtured early hopes of creating a unified, professionalized army for his conception of "New Russia," but this foundered on Moscow's half-hearted commitment to the idea of an independent Donbas state. After all, the Kremlin's goal had never been to occupy Donbas itself, but simply to use it as a lever against Kyiv; consequently, it was interested neither in outright annexation nor in supporting the creation of an independent state. Instead, its goal has been the reincorporation of a Moscow-dominated Donbas into Ukraine on its own terms, giving it the power to veto any moves by Kyiv that it dislikes.

Given their provenance and backing, the militia forces tend to field Russian-made equipment. While some is bought on the international black market, and a fair amount was taken from Ukrainian forces and arsenals at the start of the war, most is supplied by the Russians – largely from depots around the city of Rostov-on-Don, which has become a logistical and command hub for Moscow's undeclared war. The standard rifles are various versions of the 5.45mm AK-74, supplemented with RPK-74, RPK-74M and

PKM machine guns, SVD sniper rifles, and RPG rocket-grenade launchers. More advanced items, such as suppressed weapons and OSV-96 anti-matériel rifles, tend to indicate Russian *Spetsnaz* operators embedded with the militias, or particularly high-prestige individuals. The militias wear a variety of camouflage clothing, much of it commercially sourced, and few units display true uniformity of appearance and equipment.

Likewise, there is no standard organizational model, although most units use regular Russian unit nomenclature. Nonetheless, these must be taken with caution; a Russian infantry brigade has an establishment strength of 3,800 officers and men, while the LNR's Prizrak Brigade, for example, has fluctuated between around 1,000 and 3,000 effectives. Many militia units use grandiose titles such as the "Russian Orthodox Army" and the "Legion of St Stephen," but in practice most are of around battalion strength.

Their recruits come largely from the Donbas, although some units such as the Vostok Battalion (discussed below) and the Cossacks draw their fighters from other recruitment pools. The units all tend to be mixed in nature, and willing to accept whoever is willing to join. Attrition has bled away many of the experienced cadres of 2014, such as former *Berkut* riot police or veterans of the Ukrainian or Russian military. As a result, any volunteers are usually welcomed, including female combatants – this goes against the grain of the Russian military, which still generally relegates women to support roles.

The commanders of the various militia units must be acceptable to both Moscow and their local leaders, while also having the charisma or legitimacy to lead their troops. Some had a service background: for example, Alexander Khodakovsky, original commander of the Vostok Bn, was a major in the SBU's elite Alfa counter-terrorism force before defecting to the DNR, while Igor "Bes" Bezler was reportedly a lieutenant-colonel in the GRU before he retired to Ukraine in 2002. Others rose through their own talents in the chaos of the war: one, Alexander Mozgovoi, was a Cossack cook who rose no higher than senior sergeant in the Ukrainian military, but he virtually founded the Prizrak Brigade.

Alexander Zakharchenko, the "Republican Guard" and "Oplot" militia commander who rose to political and military leadership of the Donetsk People's Republic, speaking in December 2014. The blue-striped *telnyashka* vest, a symbol of Soviet and now Russian elite troops, is widely adopted by those who are neither paratroopers nor marines. Zakharchenko was killed in a café bombing on August 31, 2018. (Andrew Butko/Wikimedia Commons/ CC-BY-SA 4.0)

The Donetsk People's Militia

The Donetsk People's Militia was formally established at the very start of the war by Pavel Gubarev, the self-proclaimed "People's Governor" of Donetsk Region. Originally it had no real command structure or coordination, being simply an umbrella title for various local gangs and units. Over time, Strelkov and other figures, with the encouragement of Moscow, managed to establish some kind of meaningful structure, though this is far from being as disciplined or efficient as a regular military chain of command. It is subordinated to the DNR's prime minister, or chair of the Council of Ministers; as of December 2018 this is Denis Pushilin, a businessman regarded as receptive to Moscow's guidance. The ministers of defense, internal affairs and state security all have responsibility for certain forces, although efforts have been made to shift armed personnel from the last into the control of the Ministry of Internal Affairs.

After the first, chaotic year of the war efforts began to be made to convert semi-autonomous militias into regular units, as listed below, but to a large

Alexander Khodakovsky was a commander of the Ukrainian SBU's elite "Alfa" counter-terrorism unit who defected to the rebels and took over the DNR's Vostok Battalion. Here he is shown giving a press conference in August 2014, pointedly posing in front of a replica of the flag that men of the Soviet 150th Motor Rifle Division hoisted over the Reichstag on April 28, 1945. (*Essence of Time Official Channel/Wikimedia Commons/ CC-BY-SA 3.0*)

Rebel BMP-2 infantry fighting vehicles drive in convoy towards Donetsk in 2015. Note the brightly colored flags; turret and hull front bear white- stenciled faces of Christ and invocation "God is with us." (Mstyslav Chernov/Wikimedia Commons/CC-BY-SA 4.0)

extent this is little more than a cosmetic process. The Vostok Battalion, for example, is now officially the 11th Independent Motor Rifle Regt of the DNR's I Army Corps, but this means little on the ground. Regardless of the current official titles, many units are still more realistically considered under the sometimes fanciful names for which they are best known – and which, on the whole, they still appear to use themselves. The main units of the early DNR Militia were as follows:

Units

Republican Guard Established at the end of 2014 by Alexander Zakharchenko, and formally inducted in January 2015, this supposedly "elite" unit was considered, along with the Oplot Battalion (q.v.), to be the backstop of Zakharchenko's personal power in the DNR. Comprising six battalions, it had an establishment strength of 3,000 officers and men, although it was generally no more than two-thirds manned. Following Zakharchenko's assassination in August 2018 it experienced something of a turn-over in its command structure, with the introduction of Pushilin loyalists.

Kalmius Brigade Named after a river in the Donbas, this group is often referred to as a "special forces" unit, although it is questionable whether it merits the title; it is, however, one of the more battle-hardened militia units. It was involved in much hard fighting, especially around Donetsk and Debaltseve, and became a relatively well-organized force, albeit hardly of brigade strength; it had its own artillery company, fielding both gun and rocket systems.

Miners' Division Originally recruited from coalminers from the region, this unit was formed in summer 2014, shortly after the rebel withdrawal from Slovyansk and Kramatorsk. It was later redesignated the 4th Motor Rifle Battalion.

Oplot Brigade One of the first of the Donbas insurgent units, the Oplot ("Stronghold") Battalion, formed in mid-2014, was originally commanded by Alexander Zakharchenko himself. It was expanded into a brigade in May 2015.

Russian Orthodox Army Despite its name, this unit, founded in May 2014, is largely drawn from Ukrainian rebels, although including a number of Cossack and Russian volunteers. It has acquired an unsavory reputation, even by the standards of this war, for looting and human-rights abuses. Originally composed of perhaps a hundred fighters, its strength allegedly rose to 4,000 (although, like so many such claims, this was questionable).

Security Service Battalion Intended from the first as a sort of "Praetorian Guard," this unit was soon incorporated into the forces of the Republic State Guard Service (RGSO – see below).

Slovyansk Brigade Also called the 1st Slovyansk Brigade, this was Strelkov's own force, and from no more than a company it rose

Corps level assets:
Commandant's Independent Service Regt (Donetsk)
  Rapid Reaction Group
1st Indep Ilovaisky Guards MR (Assault) Bn "Somalia" (Donetsk) –
drawn from former Somalia and Sparta militia bns
  1st, 2nd & 3rd MR Cos
  Tank Co
Indep Recon Bn "Sparta" (Donetsk) – formerly Sparta Bn
  1st & 2nd Recon Cos
  "Lavina" ("Avalanche") Special Purpose Co
  Artillery Co
2nd Independent Tank Bn "Diesel" (Donetsk)
  1st, 2nd, 3rd & 4th Tank Cos
  1st MR Co
  Artillery Bty
  Recon Platoon
1st Indep Special Designation Bn "Khan" (Donetsk)
  1st & 2nd Spec Des Cos
3rd Indep Spec Des Bn (Donetsk)
  1st & 2nd Spec Des Cos
Indep Antiaircraft Missile Bn (Donetsk)
Azov Flotilla
  Special Unit "Typhoon"

Tactical Groups:
Tactical Group "Komsomolskoye": 1st Indep MR Bde "Slovyanskaya"
(Komsomolka) – based on Strelkov's former 1st Slovyansk Bde
  1st MR Bn "Viking", 2nd MR Bn "Semenovsky", 3rd MR Bn
  Tank Bn
  SP Artillery Bn, Artillery Bn, MLRS Bn, AT Bty
  Recon Co "Konstantinovsky"
  Engineer, Comms & Medical Cos

Tactical Group "Gorlivka": 3rd Indep MR Bde "Berkut" (Horlivka)
  1st MR Bn "Gorlivka," 2nd MR Bn "Yenakievsky," 3rd MR Bn "Lavina"
  Tank Bn
  SP Artillery Bn, Artillery Bn, MLRS Bn, AT Bty
  Recon Co
  Engineer, Comms & Medical Cos

Tactical Group "Oplot": 5th Indep MR Bde "Oplot" (Donetsk) –
based on former militia Oplot Bde
  1st & 2nd MR Bns
  1st & 2nd Tank Bns
  SP Artillery Bn, Artillery Bn, MLRS Bn, AT Bty
  Recon Co
  Engineer, Comms & Medical Cos

Tactical Group "Cupola": 100th Indep MR Bde (Donetsk) –
based on former militia Republican Guard
  1st, 2nd & 3rd MR Bns
  1st Tank Bn
  Artillery Bn, MLRS Bn, AT Bty
  Recon Co "Varyag"
  Engineer, Comms & Medical Cos

Tactical Group "Novoazovsk": 9th Indep Naval Inf Bde (Novoazovsk)
  1st MR Bn "Semyonovsky" – based on former Mariupol-Khingan
    militia regt
  2nd MR Bn
  1st Tank Bn
  SP Artillery Bn, Artillery Bn
  Engineer & Comms Cos

Tactical Group "Kolchuga": Indep Spec Des Bde "Kalmius" (Donetsk,
Snezhnoye) – based on former militia Kalmius Bde
  1st & 2nd SP Artillery Bns, MLRS Bn, AT Bn
  Security, Comms & Medical Cos

Tactical Group "Danube": 11th Indep Yenakievo-Danube MR Regt
"Vostok" (Makeyevka) – based on former Vostok Bn
  1st & 2nd MR Bns
  Tank Co
  SP Artillery Bn, Artillery Bn, MLRS Bn, Air Defense Bn
  Recon Co
  Engineer, Comms & Medical Cos

to a peak strength of 2,000 effectives, with two separate maneuver units. It was one of the more battle-ready of the DNR's forces, but its morale suffered after Strelkov's dismissal and the implicit abandonment of the notion of an independent Novorossiya. Some of its fighters defected to other militias, before it found a new identity as the DNR's 1st Independent Motor Rifle Brigade.

Somalia Battalion Sometimes also using the more grandiose title of the 1st Independent Battalion Tactical Group "Somalia," and then the 1st Independent Tank Battalion "Somalia," because it was equipped with T-64 and T-72 tanks. This unit was formerly led by LtCol Mikhail Tolstykh, known by his call sign "Givi," until his assassination in 2017. He claimed that he chose the name because its fighters were "as brave as Somalis."

Sparta Battalion Another unit whose founder fell victim to a mysterious assassination, Sparta was led by Arsen Pavlov, better known by his call sign "Motorola." This unit took part in many of the key early battles of the war, including Ilovaisk and the Second Battle for Donetsk Airport. Motorola led the unit until his death in October 2016, seeing it grow to almost 1,000 effectives.

Voskhod Battalion More properly the **Consolidated Orthodox Battalion Voskhod ("Sunrise")**, this mustered some 300 fighters. Claiming to be concerned with humanitarian protection of civilians, it actively engaged in combat operations.

The mysterious deaths of rebel commanders

The life of a "Novorossiyan" warlord is hazardous, especially if you find yourself in opposition either to your leadership or to Moscow. The year 2015 proved to be especially bloody, seeing the assassinations of the controversial LNR commanders Alexander Mozgovoi, Alexander "Batman" Bednov, and Pavel Dremov; in 2016 Arsen "Motorola" Pavlov of the DNR's Sparta Bn met the same fate, as did Mikhail Tolstykh of the Somalia Bn in 2017.

While the official line is always that they were killed by Ukrainian government Special Forces – apparently ones able to infiltrate, attack, and exfiltrate without leaving behind any evidence or ever getting caught – suspicion has fallen on Russian *Spetsnaz* or mercenaries from its Wagner Group, or, in a few cases, on rivals in the world of organized crime (such as the figures behind the gunning-down of Oplot commander Yevgeny Zhilin in a Moscow restaurant in 2016). Sometimes, however, the apparent instigator is rather closer to hand. In 2016, former LNR prime minister Gennady Tsyplakov seemingly hanged himself in prison after being accused of planning a coup against Igor Plotnitsky. His alleged co-conspirator, deputy defense minister Vitaly "Communist" Kiselyov, also died in an MGB cell, under circumstances that remain unclear. More recently, Alexander Zakharchenko, the leader of the DNR, died in a café bombing in Donetsk in August 2018 which is widely assumed to have been organized, or at least approved, by Moscow.

Vostok ("East") Brigade When the Vostok Battalion first appeared in May 2014 it was largely made up of Chechens and other veterans from the North Caucasus. They had been raised by the GRU as a means of asserting Moscow's control over the unruly Donbas militias, and their first action was indeed to take over the separatist HQ in Donetsk. However, the force was quickly "Ukrainianized" with local fighters, including veterans from *Berkut* and the former Svarog Battalion. In the process it was formally increased to a brigade, even if its actual strength rarely exceeded 1,500.

Other, smaller units came and went. The Diesel Battalion was an armored unit formed in 2015 to field tanks provided by the Russians, including

PRO-MOSCOW FORCES

(1) Militiaman, Russian Orthodox Army, 2014
This is a Donetsk militia formed in May 2014 from a mix of locals and Russian volunteers, which was initially loyal to "Strelkov" – see C3 below. It had a particularly unsavory reputation for looting and ethnic violence but was well equipped, reportedly by the FSB. This man wears Russian Army-issue battledress in Flora woodland camouflage, but his irregular status is betrayed by his privately acquired cap in Partizan camouflage and Smerch-A load-bearing rig. He displays the unit's distinctive sleeve badge, and a St George's ribbon; taped to the buttstock of his AK-74 is an image of St Alexander Nevsky, as a token of his piety.

(2) Militiaman, Prizrak Brigade, 2015
Under its former commander Alexei Mozgovoi the Prizrak or "Ghost" Bde became one of the most feared of the Luhansk units. This soldier, engaged at Debaltseve in January 2015, carries a box of 5.45mm ammunition as well as his AKS-74U carbine. Under a Smerch-AK load-bearing vest he wears a commercially sourced Gorka-4 mountain suit. The unit's subdued left-sleeve patch bears three lines of small and one of large Cyrillic script, above crossed up-curved knives, in light on darker drab green. Many recruits claimed Cossack roots; the unit is informally known as the "Antratsit Cossacks," and he wears their distinctive fleece hat, though the FC Rostov scarf suggests he may be of Russian origin.

(3) "Strelkov," 2014
Igor Girkin, widely known by the *nom de guerre* Igor Strelkov, was the defense minister of the Donetsk People's Republic between May and August 2014, and an ardent champion of the creation of "Novorossiya." He is pictured here under its flag, while giving a press conference. The insurgents' mix of government and civilian kit is evident: a civilian hunter's camouflage suit, the dated PM Makarov pistol and Soviet-era document case weighting down the map, and the modern military-issue R-168 tactical radio.

(4) Vityaz Battalion sleeve patch
The insignia of the LNR's "Knight" Bn dates from 2014, when hopes of creating a unified, independent Donbas state were still alive; it bears a "NOVOROSSIYA" scroll at the top and "LNR" at the bottom. The symbolism includes the Lugansk Region shield at the center, with a stylized forge representing its heavy industry, but this is largely a facade. Both Ukrainian intelligence and third-party analysts state that the battalion, which operated in the Krasnodon and Izvarino areas, was partially or entirely made up of Russian soldiers from the 15th Independent Motorized Brigade.

Although first fielded as long ago as 1962, the 73mm SPG-9 has seen use by militias on both sides in the Donbas war; it is especially useful against soft-skinned vehicles and static emplacements. Here, it is manned by a soldier from the DNR's 1st Motor Rifle Bde "Slovanskaya," wearing older-style Russian Flora camouflage battledress. (Gennadiy Dubovoy/Wikimedia Commons/CC-BY-SA 3.0)

T-72B1s, which later became the 2nd Tank Bn of the DNR's I Corps. By contrast, the Steppe Battalion, which probably never amounted to more than a couple of hundred Cossacks and other volunteers, appeared in June 2014 and had disbanded by the end of July, individual fighters drifting into other units or heading home. Likewise, the Semyonov Battalion became in November 2014 the Mariupol-Khingan Regt, before being rolled into the new 9th Independent Naval Infantry Brigade.

Foreign fighters who joined the DNR's ranks sometimes drifted into existing units, and sometimes formed their own (for example, the Serbian Jovan Šević Detachment, which disbanded at the end of 2014, and the picturesquely named Chechen Death Battalion, whose real role was unclear). At other times they joined the 15th International Brigade, in national detachments called "battalions" but ranging in size from 20 to a few hundred fighters. It is precisely this instability that the new military structure was intended to address.

The reformed DNR I Army Corps

By 2016, moves were already afoot under DNR defense minister Gen Vladimir Kononov (who succeeded Strelkov) to try and turn the ragtag collection of militias and private armies into a coherent fighting force, the I Army Corps (see table on page 23). Some units were folded into others or disbanded outright, their fighters being reassigned. Others were simply given new titles and places within the order of battle. A few, such as Strelkov's 1st Slovyansk Bde, survived almost untouched. The 9th Bde is even technically described as a naval infantry force, although in practice this is not reflected in its organization, training or equipment.

Beyond the regular forces of I Army Corps, the DNR deploys six Territorial Defense Battalions, which range from the relatively tough 2nd Bn, which is based on the old Miners' Division, through to the construction troops of the 3rd Battalion.

There are also the armed forces of the **Ministry of State Security (MGB)**, largely static guard personnel but including the "Zastava" special operations team; and also the armed police and security troops of the **Ministry of Internal Affairs (MVD)**. These latter include the OMON

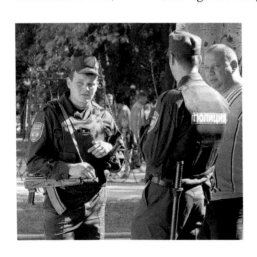

Police of the DNR in Donetsk, 2014; note the black-blue-red "national"-colored stripes forming the yellow-bordered sleeve patches, and the AKS-74U assault carbine. (Andrew Butko/Wikimedia Commons/CC-BY-SA 4.0)

riot police; SOBR police SWAT teams; and the Interior Troops, whose field force comprises the 41st and 52nd Operational Designation Regts and a *Spetsnaz* company. The separate **Republic State Guard Service (RGSO)** includes a Guard Regt with three battalions: "Patriot," "Legion," and "Vityaz" ("Knight"). However, at the time of writing, these face potentially being rolled into the forces of the MGB or MVD.

In February 2015, Zakharchenko announced that 10,000 soldiers were being mobilized, and that in due course the Donetsk People's Militia would be expanded to 100,000 strong. As with so many such claims, this boast was essentially empty. As of mid-2018 the total strength was reportedly 17,000–22,000 soldiers, of whom an estimated three-quarters were locals. According to an article in the Russian newspaper *Moskovsky komsomolets*, it could then also muster 69 venerable but still effective BM-21 Grad truck-based multiple launch rocket systems, as well as more modern equipment: 10x BM-27 Uragan, 5x BM-30 Smerch, and even 6x TOS-1 Solntsepyok thermobaric launchers. The DNR's forces are also well equipped with artillery, with self-propelled 122mm 2S1 Gvozdika and 152mm 2S3 Akatsia and 2S19 Msta-S systems, as well as towed 122mm D-30 howitzers and MT-12 Rapira antitank guns. Beyond that, they claimed to have about 400x T-64 tanks, 300x T-72s, 57x T-80s and even three T-90s. They also field BMP-1 and BMP-2 infantry fighting vehicles, and BTR-70 and -80 and MT-LB personnel carriers.

On paper, this is a truly formidable force, not least in its armored strength, but shortages of trained crews and maintenance problems mean that in practice the field force has only a fraction of that strength. Deploying the TOS-1s, for example, appears to require not just the Russians to release the rockets to the rebels, but also to provide crews, and they have yet to be used in battle. Furthermore, with the possible exception of a handful of units such as the 1st Independent Motor Rifle Bde and the Reconnaissance Bn "Sparta," few units have anything like the strength of a comparable formation in the Russian Army. Nonetheless, efforts are constantly being made to recruit more soldiers, and Moscow periodically upgrades the equipment at their disposal in response to moves on the Ukrainian side. After the USA agreed to sell Kyiv the Javelin top-attack antitank missile in 2018, for example, the Russians began transferring Shturm-S missile tank destroyer vehicles to the rebels, starting with the antitank elements of the DNR's 5th and Kalmius Brigades.

The militias on both sides have pressed a variety of improvised vehicles into service, such as this DNR gun-truck mounting a double-barrel ZU-23 cannon. Originally developed for short-range AA defense, the 23mm ZU-23 has found a second effective role as a direct-fire ground weapon. (Andrew Butko/Wikimedia Commons/CC-BY-SA 3.0)

A rebel soldier in a position near Dokuchayevsk, 2015, mans a 9K111 Fagot wire-guided antitank missile, known in the West as the AT-4 Spigot. Dating from 1970, the AT-4 is typical of the kind of second-rank equipment that the rebels could either loot from government arsenals or receive as hand-me-downs from the Russians. Nonetheless, against anything but the most modern armor it was a serious threat. (Mstyslav Chernov/Wikimedia Commons/CC-BY-SA 4.0)

The Luhansk People's Militia

With a population of only just over half that of the DNR, it is unsurprising that the LNR's forces are rather smaller, though in some cases quite effective. As with the DNR's, they emerged at first as an often haphazard array of local militias and "pocket armies." Initially most of these called themselves part of an "Army of the Southeast," but in October 2014 Igor Plotnitsky, the first LNR head of state,

Indistinct but still striking photo of an armored vehicle sergeant from the DNR's Diesel Bn looking over a captured BMP-2. Note the padded vehicle crew helmet; the dated Beryozhka camouflage battledress; the big subdued unit patch on his sleeve, and the three yellow rank bars on his shoulder tab. (Mstyslav Chernov/Wikimedia Commons/ CC-BY-SA 4.0)

formally established the People's Militia of the People's Republic of Luhansk. This force was initially commanded by Oleg Bugrov and then, from November 2014, by defense minister Sergei Ignatov. Plotnitsky stood down in November 2017, and was succeeded by minister of state security Leonid Pasechnik.

The forces of the Luhansk People's Militia have a reputation for being even less disciplined than those of Donetsk, with credible allegations of militias operating as organized criminal gangs, and frequent – and sometimes lethal – disputes between commanders. As a legacy of the initial concept of a unified Novorossiya, the LNR's forces are assembled in II Army Corps (see page 30), intended to complement the DNR's I Corps. Especially in the formative period of the Luhansk People's Militia, there was considerable cooperation and interpenetration between them and their Donetsk counterparts. For example, the 7th "Chistyakovskaya" Motor Rifle Bde is drawn in part from forces of the Slavonic Battalions, a militia which originally followed Strelkov in territory considered part of the DNR; initially an element of the latter's forces, in 2015 it transferred to the LNR. Despite these links, overall the Luhansk forces were an array of idiosyncratic local groups, often cohering around a particular region, leader or identity:

Units

Leshy ("Forest Spirit") Battalion Established in Luhansk and originally headquartered in the city's captured SBU offices, this unit was named after the call sign of its commander, Alexei Pavlov. Originally it held itself apart from the main LNR military structures, being close to Strelkov, but after he was dismissed and the Novorossiya project faded it joined the regular People's Militia. Pavlov was active in Cossack circles, and his Leshy Bn, which reached a strength of around 500 fighters by the end of 2014, recruited equally from Luhansk locals and Cossacks.

Prizrak ("Ghost") Brigade One of the most feared and effective of the militias, Prizrak also kept itself separate from the "Army of the Southeast" and even from LNR People's Militia command structures, at least until the mysterious assassination of its commander, Alexander Mozgovoi, in 2015. It recruited heavily from Cossacks, and its reputation also helped attract volunteers from abroad. Most of these went into its largely French-speaking Continental Unit, and into Unit 404, a detachment of foreign communist fighters also known as the Biryukov-Markov Unit.

Rus Battalion Initially this was formed by several hundred workers and security guards from the Krasnodonuglya mine complex; it was later incorporated into the 4th Brigade.

Zarya ("Dawn") Battalion One of the largest, best-organized and disciplined of the LNR militias, founded by Igor Plotnitsky, it was raised in Luhansk itself and took its name from the local football team. In due course it would become the core of the 2nd Bde of II Army Corps.

Cossack National Guard, Great Host of the Don Cossacks, & First Cossack Regiment Like Mozgovoi's Prizrak Bde, the various Cossack units, drawn from both Ukraine and southern Russia, considered themselves allied rather than subordinated to the LNR's chain of command.

Valery Bolotov (center), briefly leader of the Luhansk People's Republic, declares independence from Kyiv in May 2014, flanked by vigilant guards from the former *Berkut* riot police. A paratroop veteran turned businessman, Bolotov headed the LNR for just three months before resigning. Aged 46, he died at his home in Moscow in January 2017, ostensibly of natural causes. (Che Guevara YouTube Channel/Wikimedia Commons/ CC-BY-SA 3.0)

The Cossack National Guard, based at Antratsit and originally commanded by *Ataman* Nikolai Kozitsyn, was the largest, with over 4,000 fighters at its peak. The First Cossack Regiment was a splinter group based at Stakhanov, which separated because of personal disagreements between Kozitsyn and its founder, Pavel Dryomov. The Great Host of the Don Cossacks was more of a political umbrella organization, active in attracting recruits, but it did maintain some small combat units of its own.

Rapid Reaction Group "Batman" Another unit whose name derives from the *nom de guerre* of its original leader, this was established by Alexander "Batman" Bednov, a former Soviet riot policeman. Initially it was part of the People's Militia, but in summer 2014 Bednov declared its independence; his force by then numbered over 400, and included the so-called "Kornilovtsy" and "Rusich" Independent Assault Groups of Russian ultra-nationalists. Even by the standards of this vicious war, the unit acquired a troubling reputation for looting, organized criminality and human-rights abuses.

Rebels at a checkpoint in 2015. Note the mix of equipment and uniforms characteristic of that time; the men at left and center wear old Russian winter-weight uniforms in Flora camouflage and a SSh-40 steel helmet, while their colleague on the right has digital EMR camouflage and a modern polymer 6B27 helmet. (Photo by Pierre Crom/Getty Images)

Corps level assets:
Commandant's Indep Service Regt of People's Militia (Luhansk)
Indep Recon Bn (Stakhanov) – includes 3rd Stanichno-Luhansk Assault Bn
4th Indep Spec Des Bn – incl. elements of Batman Rapid Reaction Group
Indep SAM Bn (Luhansk)
Indep Comms Bn (Luhansk)

Brigades:
2nd Guards Order of Valor MR Bde "Voroshilov" (Luhansk) – based on Zarya Bde
    1st, 2nd (incl. Hooligan Bn) & 3rd MR Bns
    Tank Bn
    SP Artillery Bn

4th Guards MR Brigade (Krasny Luch) – based on Leshy Bn
    1st, 2nd (based on Rus & Vityaz Bns) & 3rd (incl. elements of Batman RR Group) MR Bns

Brigade Artillery Group, MLRS Bty, AT Bty
Recon Co (based on elements of Batman RR Group)

7th Indep MR Bde "Chistyakovskaya" (Debaltseve & Bryanka)
    1st "Slavic," 2nd "Semyonovsky" & 3rd MR Bns
    Brigade Artillery Group, Air Defense Group

1st Indep Cossack MR Regt "Ataman Platov" (Alchevsk)
    1st (based on Cossack Nat Gd), 2nd & 3rd (based on 1st Cossack Regt) MR Bns
    Artillery Bn

Indep Spec Des Artillery Bde
1st Indep Guards Tank Bn "August" (Luhansk) – based on militia unit of that name
Territorial Defense Battalions

Associated forces:
Prizrak Mech Bde/ 4th TD Bde (Alchevsk)

Under investigation by the LNR's general prosecutor, Bednov brought his unit back into the fold (the militants of "Rusich" left in disgust, although the "Kornilovtsy" stayed). However, Bednov's obvious political ambitions, brutal methods, and criminal enterprises made him many enemies. In January 2015 his convoy was ambushed and he was killed in a hail of grenades and gunfire. His unit was then divided amongst other elements of II Corps (see above).

USSR Battalion For a while this militia unit essentially controlled the town of Bryanka, west of Luhansk, under its commander Denis Pindyurin (who went by the call sign "Fierce"). In due course it was essentially incorporated into the LNR structure, its soldiers moving into the Territorial Defense Battalions.

1st Independent "August" Tank Battalion The only dedicated armored unit in the LNR forces, this has essentially transitioned to the new structure; in the process many of its initial T-64s, including a few Ukrainian-variant Bulats, have been replaced with T-72Bs supplied by Russia.

3rd Stanichno-Luhansk Assault Battalion A force drawn largely from former paratroopers, including middle-aged veterans of the Soviet war in Afghanistan, this was thus prized for its reconnaissance fieldcraft.

Again, there were also more transient and local militias, such as the Hooligan Battalion which became part of the 2nd Brigade, and Brigade S, actually no more than a company in size. The Krasnodon Peresvet Detachment became the Vityaz Battalion when it reached company size, and was in due course rolled into the 4th Brigade. Some, however, remained outside the main II Corps organization; for example, the Alexander Nevsky Battalion joined the Prizrak Brigade.

Luhansk II Army Corps

The field force of the LNR, II Army Corps, is also known as the Luhansk Tactical Operational Group, although such terms have little real meaning. Less extensive and in the main less heavily equipped than that of Donetsk, the formation comprises three brigades, plus a "Cossack" Regt and the maverick Prizrak Brigade. Technically known since 2015 as the 4th Territorial Defense Brigade, the latter remains a semi-detached formation, within the LNR chain of command yet periodically asserting its autonomy. Overall, the LNR can field an estimated 9,000–13,000 fighters.

The LNR's forces also include other territorial defense "brigades," frequently little more than local home guard forces with widely varying strengths and levels of training and equipment; for example, the 13th "Kulki" Territorial Defense Bn from Rovenki is closer to a company in size. Even as late as 2017 some fighters were still seen carrying not just older AK-47s, but semi-automatic SKS carbines dating back to the 1950s, and even World War II-vintage PPSh SMGs.

Overall, the equipment of the Luhansk People's Militia is, like the DNR's, a mixture of dated weapons looted from Ukrainian Army stocks, equally dated kit supplied by Russia, and a smaller proportion of more modern weapons and vehicles that the Kremlin deemed necessary to help redress the balance with government forces. The T-72Bs deployed by the 1st Tank Bn, for example, are not up to the standard of the more advanced Russian T-27B3s, but they are an upgraded version not made or used in Ukraine, so could not have been captured locally. Many "mechanized" motor rifle units depend on trucks or modified and armed "technicals" (pick-ups), as well as BTR and MT-LB personnel carriers, with relatively few BMP infantry fighting vehicles. Artillery is still primarily 2S1 Gvozdika and 2S3 Akatsiya self-propelled guns, although they field at least one 152mm 2S5 Gyatsint-S gun, along with towed D-30 pieces. They have a few BM-27 Uragan MLRS, but appear not to possess the more modern systems provided to the DNR.

RUSSIAN REGULAR FORCES

From the very start of the conflict Russian regular forces have played a central part. In Crimea, the role of the "self-defense volunteers" was essentially cosmetic. In the Donbas, Moscow sought to rely on militias as much as possible, but even so political and Special Forces operators, deniable military advisers, and other Russian assets were involved from the first. From autumn 2014, when it became clear that the rebel militias could not stand up to the Ukrainian government forces, Moscow has had to maintain both forces within the Donbas and also large strategic reserves ready to be surged into the warzone as and when they may be needed. In engagements such as the

Pro-Kyiv volunteers take a moment for a photo during the defense of Debaltseve in September 2014; the rebel counter-offensive the following winter would demonstrate the decisive importance of regular Russian artillery support. Note (center) the three-fingered national salute evoking Ukraine's *tryzub* trident symbol. The very random assortment of camouflage clothing and equipment, as well as the elderly AK-47s they carry, are typical of the first year of the war. (VO Svoboda/Wikimedia Commons/CC-BY-SA 3.0)

The T-72 tank was introduced as long ago as 1973, but nonetheless has proven strikingly "future-proof". The latest T-72B3 version, with better fire control and more effective reactive armor, is the mainstay of Russian regular armored units in the Donbas. (Ministry of Defence of the Russian Federation/Mil.ru/Wikimedia Commons/CC-BY-SA 4.0)

fateful battle of Debaltseve the presence of Russian troops, and especially Russian artillery, has proven decisive.

The battle of Debaltseve

The city of Debaltseve is strategically vital, being located between the territories held by the DNR and LNR, as well as being a key road and rail hub on the way to Artemivsk and Slovyansk – two rebel objectives. Rebels seized it in April 2014, but it was recaptured by Kyiv's troops in July. As a result, it was at the heart of a pocket of government-held territory wedged between the two rebel regions.

In January 2015, in tough winter conditions and supported by a heavy artillery barrage, the rebels launched an offensive to capture the city. Government forces resisted, and in the ensuing artillery duel soldiers and civilians alike were killed in significant numbers. As rebel forces encircled

RUSSIAN FORCES

(1) Infantryman with RPG-29, 2016

This Russian soldier steadies his RPG-29 "Vampir" antitank rocket launcher during the fighting at Zaitseve in April 2016. He wears winter battledress in Flora camouflage, and although he displays no insignia he is probably from the 19th Independent Motor Rifle Brigade. For personal self-defense he carries a slung AKS-7U carbine.

(2) Tank crewman, 2016

Probably a soldier of the tactical group drawn from the 136th Indep Guards MR Bde, he hails from Buinaksk in Dagestan. Originally deployed to Luhansk in 2014, elements of the 136th returned in 2016. This soldier can be dated to the later deployment by his kit: in the interim they had traded their dated Soviet-era KLMK coveralls in Beryozhka-pattern camouflage for this latest 6B15 equipment. Known as "cowboy" kit, it includes body armor over flame-resistant coveralls, which incorporate a hood over the usual padded vehicle helmet with integral intercom headset. While most

Russian tanks in the Donbas have been T-72B3s, the 136th is equipped with the T-90A.

(3) Junior lieutenant combat medic, Airborne Forces, 2017

The Russian armed forces still lag behind in the resources they invest in medical services, but they are seeking to make up for this historical weakness. This paratrooper combat medic – a junior lieutenant, to judge by the single star on his shoulder straps – is probably from the 333rd Abn Regt of the 98th Airborne Brigade. As well as his medical bag and a folding stretcher he carries a slung AK-74, as is standard Russian practice. He wears a 6Sh92 tactical vest over his Flora-pattern paratroop uniform.

(4) 200th Motor Rifle Brigade sleeve patch

Since 2011 this formation, based in the northern city of Pechenga, has been one of Russia's specialist Arctic-warfare units – note the polar bear and icecap symbolism here. The deployment of battalion tactical groups from the Arctic all the way to the Donbas since 2014 is evidence of the lengths to which Moscow has been forced to go to find high-quality professional troops for such missions.

On the modern battlefield electronic warfare often shapes its kinetic counterpart. The Russians have deployed many of their advanced EW assets to Ukraine, including this 1RL257E Krasukha-4 broadband radar jammer. (Ministry of Defense of the Russian Federation/Mil.ru/ Wikimedia Commons/CC-BY-SA 4.0)

Debaltseve, ceasefires brokered by outside forces came to nothing. Attempts by Kyiv to relieve the 6,000 government troops in this "kettle" were largely aborted by the volume of artillery fire they faced, and it soon became clear that much of this was being delivered by a Russian force drawn from the 8th and 18th Guards MR Bdes and the 232nd Rocket Bde, while the 25th *Spetsnaz* Regt provided both assault troops and artillery spotters. A battalion tactical group based on Russia's 136th Guards MR Bde was also leading efforts to close the road corridor into the city, suffering sufficient losses that it had to be replaced with another from the 27th Guards MR Bde and the 217th Guards Abn Regt (from the 98th Guards Airborne Division). Ukrainian forces were eventually forced to withdraw under heavy fire on February 18, leaving behind a shattered city – and also a lesson to the world as to the scale of direct Russian involvement, and the degree to which this could tip the balance.

Build-up of forces

In August 2014 the Russians deployed an estimated 3,500–6,500 troops into Ukraine, growing to a peak of some 10,000 by the end of that year. First of all, reconnaissance and sabotage detachments from the 2nd and 10th *Spetsnaz* Bdes, the 106th Guards Abn Div, the 45th Guards Abn *Spetsnaz* Regt, and the 9th and 18th MR Bdes were deployed to prepare the ground. Then, the first wave of regular combat forces saw the introduction of battalion tactical groups (BTGs, discussed below) – composite units drawn from fully ten maneuver units: the 17th, 18th and 21st MR Bdes, 33rd (Mountain) MR Bde, 31st Guards Air Assault Bde, 2nd *Spetsnaz* Bde, 104th and 247th Air-Assault Regts, and the 137th and 331st Airborne Regiments.

Although the precise numbers have fluctuated, Moscow has since maintained around 10,000 troops in the Donbas for most of the war, but this is by no means the limit of the Russian commitment. Almost 30,000 troops, including 13,000 in the Black Sea Fleet, are based in Crimea, and could be used for direct incursions into Ukraine. More broadly, Russia maintains not just Army but also FSB Border Guard forces along and close to the Ukrainian border. The numbers again vary, but they peak during military exercises at around 75,000. Thus, of a total Ground Forces field strength of 350,000, Moscow keeps almost a quarter directly engaged in the Donbas or within easy deployment range.

This is not without significant cost. To generate the estimated 42,000 personnel rotated through or near the Donbas in 2014 meant drawing on some 117 combat and combat-support units. "Scratch-built" BTGs are required to enable Russia to field substantial operational forces in the Donbas itself, and this has meant pulling in troops from all over the country, including marines from the Far North, mechanized infantry from the Far East, and elite troops from every single *Spetsnaz* and paratroop formation. On the one hand, these deployments have had some undoubted benefits: they allow a new generation of soldiers and junior officers to gain proper combat experience, and provide an opportunity to test out new equipment and tactics. This has, however, been at the expense of considerable pressure on the military structure, and the inevitable costs of moving units and their equipment back and forth across the largest country in the world.

Command and control
Although a variety of other agencies are also involved, such as the FSB and even the Ministry of Emergency Situations (which has run numerous convoys into the Donbas, notionally delivering humanitarian aid, but which many believe also provide resupply to fighters), overall responsibility for the Russian aspect of the Donbas war rests with the General Staff and the newly built National Defense Control Center in the basement of the Defense Ministry building. That said, it is important to stress that they do not have direct operational command over the militias. Some, at least in the past, have been essentially Russian-run, such as the Vostok Battalion. Some, again, are more beholden to Moscow than others, or are in effect attached to Russian BTGs as local auxiliaries on an operation-by-operation basis. But command and control, and coordination, have been perennial challenges: the Kremlin has traded off operational effectiveness for the sake of deniability.

The formidable TOS-1A Solntsepyok (nicknamed *Buratino*, "Pinocchio") is an MLRS firing 24x 220mm thermobaric munitions. While the Russians may have provided some to the DNR forces, by all accounts they maintain close control over their use, even withholding the rockets until they are willing to see them deployed. (Vitaly V. Kuzmin/Wikimedia Commons/ CC-BY-SA 4.0)

A Russian *Spetsnaz* operator from the 22nd Special Designation Bde, based in the Rostov region. He carries both a regular assault rifle slung, and an AS Val suppressed rifle. (Ministry of Defense of the Russian Federation/Mil.ru/ CC-BY-SA 4.0)

The Russian city of Rostov-on-Don, capital of the Rostov region and an important seaport and road and rail hub, has become the logistical base for the undeclared war in the Donbas. Not only does it house arsenals and warehouses with weapons and other matériel to support Russian and rebel forces, but the GRU maintains a significant presence there. Potential volunteers and mercenaries for the militias are screened, armed, and mustered in the city, while analysts draw on a network of human and electronic intelligence assets to try to maintain a real-time sense of this messiest of conflicts.

The Eighth Guards Army, which was re-formed in 2017, is based south of Rostov-on-Don, at Novorossisk. Although the Twentieth Guards Army at Voronezh to the north certainly also plays a role in the threatening force posture that Moscow presents, the Eighth appears to have been made the operational hub for deployments into the Donbas, while it also poses the main conventional threat to Ukraine. However, its role is complicated by the multiple institutions with a role in the overall mission.

Politically, the Presidential Administration in Moscow is running the show, for most of the time through presidential aide Vladislav Surkov. His is very much a diplomatic and administrative mission, but nonetheless this feeds directly into combat operations – in terms of when to observe and when to ignore ceasefires, when to step up the tempo of fire missions to put pressure on Kyiv, or when to calm them down to appease third parties. Meanwhile, both the GRU and the Federal Security Service (FSB) – which is technically a domestic security agency, but has been engaged in active empire-building – have their clients amongst the militias, and the FSB also has so-called "curators," political agents, in both Donetsk and Luhansk. They have their own ideas on how the war should be fought, as well as differing agendas in Moscow. Furthermore, while command of *Spetsnaz*

E **RUSSIAN FORCES**
(1) FSB Border Guard, 2016
The FSB's Border Troops played an active role in securing and controlling the Russian-Ukrainian frontier alongside the Donbas. This officer – his status evident from the badge on his green beret, and the fact that he carries a holstered pistol as well as his rifle – is manning a checkpoint along Highway E-50 into the Donbas. He thus wears minimal equipment over his elderly "amoeba-pattern" camouflage coverall; however, the AK-74 with attached GP-34 grenade launcher is a reminder of the local upsurge in violence, which has seen the murder rate soar in neighboring Rostov-on-Don.

(2) *Spetsnaz* **operator, 2017**
This specialist is preparing an ambush in northwestern Donbas, with a MON-50 "Claymore"-style directional anti-personnel mine. His weapon is the 9mm Vintorez SVV suppressed sniper rifle. Over his Spekter-S camouflage overalls and LBV tactical vest he wears a personally fashioned "ghillie suit"; this is based on an olive-green hooded and sleeved cape, with many external loops for attaching strips of "scrim."

His footwear is decidedly non-regulation, and characterizes the latitude granted to *Spetsnaz* in the field.
(3) APC driver, Vostok Battalion, 2015–16
Although quickly "Ukrainianized" with locals, when the Vostok ("East") Bn first arrived in Donetsk in May 2014 it was largely made up of volunteers from Russia's Northern Caucasus – tough veterans of the Chechen Wars. This more recent recruit, the driver of a BTR-70 personnel carrier, presents a thoroughly mixed image: a knotted bandana in place of a cap, Russian Army Flora-pattern trousers with a store-bought camouflage T-shirt, an M32 tactical rig, a holstered PYa pistol, plus a bead bracelet and running shoes.

(4) 14th Special Designation Brigade sleeve patch
This *Spetsnaz* formation, usually based at Ussurisk in the Russian Far East, deployed elements to the Ukrainian border late in 2014. Its unit patch combines the parachute and bat symbol of the GRU with a lightning bolt; this alludes to its role as a commando unit which saw action in the Soviet-Afghan and both Chechen Wars. The inscription reads "SPETSNAZ KDVO," the latter being the abbreviation of the Red Banner Far Eastern Military District.

Drones such as this *Forpost* (a license-produced version of the IMI Searcher II, with both radar and optical sensors) have given the Russians a particular advantage over Kyiv's forces. (Vitaly V. Kuzmin/Wikimedia Commons/CC-BY-SA 4.0)

troops in the field is an operational matter, formally they are subordinated to the GRU rather than local commanders.

As if this were not complex enough, Moscow has also experimented with mercenary units in the Donbas. (This, in addition to the many individuals fighting in the DNR and LNR militias for money rather than conviction.) A force known as the Wagner Group (*Grupa Vagnera*) was founded in 2014 – even though private military companies were not at the time legal in Russia – and was deployed into the Donbas as an additional force, both to stiffen and support the militias and to assert Moscow's authority over them. Commanded by an ex-*Spetsnaz* lieutenant-colonel, Dmitry Utkin (call sign "Wagner"), the firm is registered in Argentina to get around Russian law, but has its HQ at Molkino on the base of the 10th *Spetsnaz* Brigade. Before later being deployed to Syria, and then to other theaters including the Central African Republic, Wagner was active largely within the LNR, including during the battle for Debaltseve. It is also claimed that it was employed to eliminate militia commanders whom Moscow mistrusted. Either way, its chain of command has always been unclear, but undoubtedly stretched directly to Moscow rather than to Eighth Army or the Rostov-on-Don staff.

Battalion Tactical Groups

About half Russia's soldiers are conscripts, which has posed some particular political and operational challenges for Moscow. By law, conscripts may not serve in military operations abroad except when a war has formally been declared, unless they volunteer. Even if they do choose to do so, their compulsory military service lasts for just 12 months, and after completing basic and unit training they are typically only considered truly useful for three or at most four months of their term. Furthermore, there has (rightly) been considerable discomfort in the Kremlin about the potential backlash from ordinary Russians if conscripts begin to die in a war that officially isn't being fought.

As a result, the Army opted to create composite battalion tactical groups – "modular" forces typically drawn from all-volunteer companies and battalions in existing brigades. This poses some difficulties while soldiers unused to fighting together adjust to their new structures, but it has meant that the Russians can deploy meaningfully-sized field forces drawn wholly from *kontraktniki* – professionals who are both better trained than conscripts, and also legally deployable abroad.

The BTGs vary, their structure (see page 40) reflecting both operational needs and available personnel, but in general they are mechanized battalions 300–500 strong, with two to four tank or mechanized infantry companies, and attached artillery, reconnaissance, engineer, electronic warfare and rear support platoons. For example, at Aleysk in the Altai region between Kazakhstan and Mongolia, the Forty-First Army's 35th Indep MR Bde formed the basis of a BTG with one T-90 tank company, three mechanized companies, a battery of self-propelled guns and another of MLRS systems, as well as support units. Another BTG, based on the Fifty-Eighth Army's 19th MR Bde from Vladikavkaz in North Ossetia, included a mechanized company in BMP-3 infantry fighting vehicles, another in BTR-82As, a tank company with T-90s, a battery of Msta-S SPGs, a battery of Tornado-G MLRS, a drone company, and an oversized sniper platoon drawn from another brigade.

The result is a fairly self-sufficient ground combat unit with disproportionate fire and rear support, in some ways a scaled-down version of the brigades which are the basic building block of the Russian Army. Nonetheless, as noted above, the need to rotate BTGs through the Donbas to replace casualties, resupply, and allow soldiers necessary R&R, does mean that maintaining enough such units is a massive personnel and logistical challenge, pulling in troops from all across Russia.

Arms and equipment
The forces deployed into the Donbas have on the whole been the best at Russia's disposal, even if the need to keep rotating the BTGs has sometimes made this difficult. They are typically units which have benefited from the money Putin has spent on military modernization (total security spending, including the intelligence and security services, regularly accounts for 25–35 percent of the total federal budget[3]). That policy has sometimes been slightly moderated by security concerns over the risk of some of the latest equipment – notably advanced communications systems, such as the Sagittarius battle-management computer – falling into enemy hands. Thus, while the new *Ratnik* personal uniform and equipment suite has not been deployed fully, in the main the conflict has seen Moscow testing out its best and latest kit.

Most Russian troops are still equipped with the 5.45mm AKM-74 assault rifle and the SVD sniper rifle, but rarer weapons such as the ASS Val and VSS Vintorez silenced rifles and ASVK sniper rifle are also used by specialist units. Re-usable and one-shot RPG rocket launchers are also widely used, along with mortars and grenade launchers. The soldiers are equipped with Barmitsa 6B11, 6B12, 6B13 and later 6B21 body armor, composite helmets, and modern communications systems.

Along with MT-LB and BTR-80, -82A and -90 armored personnel carriers, troops have been observed in BMP-2 and -3 infantry fighting vehicles, as well as some Gaz-233014 Tigr infantry mobility vehicles. Some T-90A tanks have been fielded, but the mainstay of Russian armored forces in the Donbas has been the latest iteration of the T-72, the T-72B3, with

3 See Elite 217, *The Modern Russian Army 1992–2016*

Kontakt-5 explosive reactive armor, an advanced fire control system, the Sosna-U gunner's sight with thermal imaging, and the capacity to launch AT-11 Svir or Refleks missiles through its 125mm gun.

A crucial Russian strength, that of its artillery, has been especially evident in the Donbas, where massed modern systems, often using new drone-based spotting capabilities, have been responsible for some key successes. On July 11, 2014, for example, after multiple fly-overs by Russian Orlan-10 drones, convoys from the Ukrainian 24th and 72nd Mech Bdes and the 79th Airmobile Bde were targeted near the village of Zelenopillya by Tornado-G MLRSs, an advanced version of the dated BM-21 issued to the rebels. Forty salvoes were fired from inside Russian territory, with high accuracy: 37 soldiers were killed and almost 100 wounded, and a stretch of road was left littered with burnt-out trucks and armor. Most of the artillery tubes deployed are self-propelled – the 122mm 2S1 Gvozdika, 152mm 2S3 Akatsiya, 2S5 Giatsint-S and 2S19 Msta-S, as well as 2S23 Nona-SVK 120mm gun-mortar – but some 122mm 2A18 D-30 and 152mm 2A36 Giatsint-B towed howitzers have also been seen, along with 2A29 MT-12 Rapira antitank guns. A full array of wheeled and tracked MLRS systems has also been used: the 122mm Tornado-G, 220mm BM-27 Uragan, 300mm BM-30 Smerch and TOS-1 thermobaric launcher.

The use of drones has been particularly noteworthy, as the Russians make strides to catch up with Western practice. As well as the Orlan, they have used the Granat-1 and -2, the Forpost, the Eleron 3SV, the Zastava (an Israeli-built BirdEye 400), and the hand-launched ZALA-421–08 for observation and fire control. This has helped make up for the Russians'

TYPICAL RUSSIAN BATTALION TACTICAL GROUP

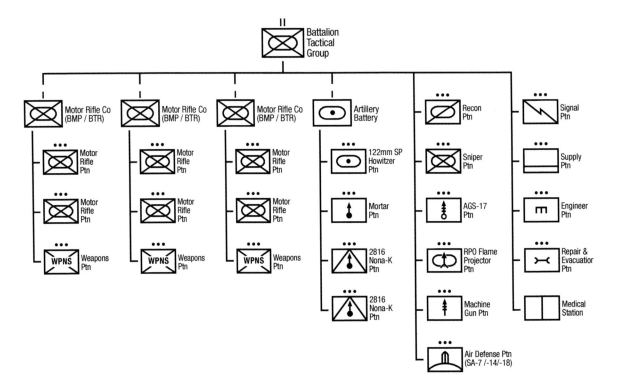

decision not to use their considerable superiority in conventional air power, both to preserve a modicum of deniability but also because it is certain that they would suffer losses if deployed in combat. As well as using drones, they have also appreciated the need to combat them. Ukraine has relatively few, but the Organization for Security and Cooperation in Europe (OSCE) – which has been trying, often vainly, to monitor breaches of the Minsk Accords and the many short-term ceasefires – has found the quadcopter drones it uses shot down, or rendered useless by jamming. Ukraine's drones face the same problems.

Although Ukraine has made little use of its Air Force, the potential threat has meant that although BTGs tend to be lighter in anti-air firepower than artillery support, Russian forces have been observed not only carrying Strela-3 (SA-14) and Igla-S (SA-24) man-portable surface-to-air missiles, but also supported by Strela-10 (SA-13) missile carriers and Pantsir-S1 (SA-22) vehicles carrying both 30mm autocannon and missiles. Since the notorious shooting down of the MH17 airliner no Buk (SA-11) medium-range systems appear to have been deployed, although there are many along the border, but in any case the airspace over the Donbas is also controlled by long-range S-300 (SA-12) missiles based inside Russia.

This is a war in which surveillance and C3I (command, control, communications, and intelligence) are of vital importance. The Russians have deployed SNAR-10 Leopard battlefield surveillance radars, ARK-1 Lynx artillery radars and Zoopark-1 counter-battery radars, as well as such advanced electronic warfare systems as the 1RL243 Rubikon signals intelligence station and the latest RB-341V Leer-3 jammer, only introduced in 2015. R-441 Liven mobile satellite communications provide secure communications between Moscow, Rostov-on-Don, and operational headquarters in the Donbas.

UKRAINIAN REGULAR FORCES

Russia's success in taking Crimea virtually without a shot being fired, and the apparent disarray of Ukrainian security forces when faced with the weaponized chaos of the Donbas, seems to have led Moscow into an initial belief that Ukraine could be intimidated into compliance easily. This was to prove a serious underestimation of both the capacities of the new government, and the public's commitment to defending its newly reaffirmed sovereignty. Indeed, given the dysfunction of so much of the rest of the government, it is striking how quickly Ukraine's armed forces were able to regroup, even if they did often have to depend on contributions and support from civil society. Overall, the war has pushed long-overdue defense reform, seeing an increasing effort to model the Ukrainian military on its NATO counterparts, assisted by support from many Western nations in everything from training to equipment.

A bitter legacy
In 2014, the Ukrainian military was still to a great extent living under the shadow of its Soviet predecessor. At the end of 1991, when the USSR was dismantled, Kyiv assumed control of those legacy forces on its territory: the

Soldiers from Ukraine's 28th Mech Bde advance alongside their BMP-2 infantry fighting vehicle in 2017, their modern uniforms and body armor demonstrating the changes that had taken place since the start of the war. (Public Domain/Sgt Anthony Jones)

Carpathian, Kiev and Odessa Military Districts, four Air Armies, the 8th Air Defense Army, five armies, and an army corps. Most of the Black Sea Fleet was based in Ukrainian ports, but in the eventual 1997 agreement which saw it divided most went to Russia. Likewise, by agreement the nuclear weapons of the 19th and 46th Rocket Divisions were later repatriated to Russia.

This meant that Ukraine inherited some 780,000 personnel (or at least, units with that "paper" strength), 6,500 tanks, 7,000-plus other armored vehicles, 1,500 combat aircraft and a fleet of 350 ships. As befits a frontline region of the Soviet military, it also had more than 7 million guns and 2.5 million tons of ammunition, stored in over 180 arsenals and bases. However, the new country lacked both the money to pay and maintain such a military, and any sense that that would be necessary, with Russia now ostensibly a friend (and itself in disarray).

Through the 1990s this massive structure withered. Young men simply failed to answer the draft, weapons were stolen, and bases and equipment

Table 5: Ukrainian forces committed to the ATO, 2016*

(*Note: Some more recent deployments are shown on Ground Forces/Operational Commands map for 2017 on page 47.)

Joint Anti-Terrorism Operational Headquarters (Kyiv)
48th Indep Engineering Bde (Pokrovskoye, Bakhmutka)
12th Indep Engineering Regt (Popasna)

Ground Forces:
10th Indep Mtn Assault Bde (Marinka-Krasnohorivka)
    8th Indep Inf Bn (Krasnohorivka)
    24th Indep Assault Bn "Aydar" (Taramchuk)
14th Indep Mech Bde (Shastya)
24th Indep Mech Bde (Novoaydar)
28th Indep Mech Bde (Stanychno)
30th Indep Mech Bde (Novohrad-Volynsky)
53rd Indep Mech Bde (Horlivka and Toretsk)
    43rd Indep Mech Inf Bn (Avdiivka)
54th Indep Mech Bde (Bakhmut)
    25th Indep Bn "Kyivan Rus" (Svitlodarsk)
56th Indep Mot Inf Bde (Myrne)
    21st Indep Mech Inf Bn (Pavlopil, Volovakha)
    23rd Indep Mech Inf Bn (Pavlopil)
    37th Indep Mot Inf Bn (Hnutovo, Volovakha)
57th Indep Mech Bde (Horlivka)
    42nd Indep Mot Bn (Horlivka)
    34th Territorial Defense Bn "Fatherland" (Zaitseve)
    17th Indep Mech Inf Bn (Zaitseve)
58th Indep Mot Inf Bde (Avdiivka)
    13th Indep Mech Inf Bn (Yasinuvatska)
    15th Indep Mech Inf Bn (Verhnetoretsk)
    16th Indep Mech Inf Bn (Avdiivka)
59th Indep Mech Inf Bde (Marinka)
    9th Indep Mech Inf Bn (Popasna)
    10th Indep Mech Inf Bn (?)
    11th Indep Mech Inf Bn (Popasna)
72nd Indep Mech Bde (Volnovakha)
    14th Indep Mech Inf Bn (Volnovakha)
92nd Indep Mech Bde (Bashkyryvka)
93rd Indep Mech Bde, Butivka (Cherkaske)
    20th Indep Mech Inf Bn (Pisky)
    39th Indep Mech Inf Bn (Avdiivka)
128th Mtn Inf Bde (Avdiivka, Krasnohorivka, Piskiy & Opitne)
    15th Indep Mtn Inf Bn (Butivka)
1st Indep Tank Bde (Krasnoarmiysk & Horlivka)

17th Indep Tank Bde (Krivy Rih)
26th Indep Artillery Bde (Berdychiv)
40th Indep Artillery Bde (Volnovokha)
44th Indep Artillery Bde (Severodonetsk)
55th Indep Artillery Bde (Avdiivka)
3rd Indep Special Purpose Rgt (*location unknown*)
54th Indep Recon Bn (*location unknown*)
74th Indep Recon Bn (*location unknown*)

Air Assault Forces:
79th Indep Air-Assault Bde (Marinka)
80th Indep Air-Assault Bde (Avdiivka)
81st Indep Airmobile Bde (Avdiivka & Pisky)
    90th Indep Airmobile Bn (Avdiivka)
    122nd Indep Airmobile Bn (Novgorodske)

Air Force:
40th Tactical Aviation Bde (Shastya)
96th Air Defense Bde (Artemivsk)

Navy:
36th Indep Naval Inf Bde (Shyrokyne, Mariupol)
    501st Indep Naval Inf Bn (Mariupol)
73rd Naval Special Operations Center (Dokuchayevsk)

National Guard:
3rd Operational Bde (Kharkiv)
5th Indep NG Bde "Slobozhanska" (Kharkiv)
15th Indep NG Regt (Sloviansk)
18th Operational Regt (Reinforced) (Mariupol)
11th Indep NG Bn (Sumy)
Special Designation Intelligence Detachment "Ares" (Kharkiv)
Front Line Bn Tactical Group "Donbas" ("Right Sector")
(Luhanske & Avdiivka)

Special Police units:
Regt "Dnipro-1" (Dnipropetrovsk)
Bn "Kharkiv" (Kharkiv)
Bn "Kherson" (Kherson)
Bn "Luhansk-1" (Dnipropetrovsk)
Bn "Mykolaiv" (Mykolaiv)
Bn "Sichyeslav" (Dnipropetrovsk)
Bn "Skif" (Zaporizhiya)
Bn "Storm" (Odesa)

---

decayed into disrepair. Desperate both to reduce its bloated inventory and to earn some income, the state sold what it could (including the rusting hulk of the incomplete Kuznetsov-class aircraft carrier *Varyag*, which ultimately became China's first carrier, the *Liaoning*). At the end of 1996 a new State Program for the Construction and Development of the Armed Forces of Ukraine was adopted, which focused above all on bringing the defense budget down to something Kyiv could afford.

Most divisions became brigades, subordinated to three Operational Commands (Western, Southern, and Northern), with some elite forces such as the 1st Airmobile Div kept as strategic assets. Given that Ukraine had been home to a substantial share of the Soviet defense-industrial complex, efforts were also stepped up to use these to develop new systems (or more often, indigenized variants of old ones) both for domestic use and export. Thus, the T-84 Oplot emerged as an updated variant of the Soviet T-80; and the BTR-94 was a short-lived version of the BTR-80 that was only ever bought by Jordan (which ordered 50, and eventually passed them on to Iraq).

By 2003 the Ukrainian military had been downsized to 295,000 personnel, some of whom were relatively competent, others less so. Detachments had served in such international peace-keeping missions as UNPROFOR in the former Yugoslavia, and KFOR and UNMIK in Kosovo, with mixed results. The international financial crisis in 2008 further increased the pressures on the armed forces, and by 2010 their total strength was down to 200,000 – of whom 41,000 were civilian employees. When Viktor Yanukovych was elected president in 2011 he presided over a further reduction of military strength, including the ending of conscription in 2013. At the time, the military was 60 percent professional and 40 percent conscripted; although funds were allocated to trying to attract more volunteers, the result was inevitable contraction in the short term.

Neither was this just a question of numbers. Funds for training and exercises had been squeezed; maintenance problems would continue to bedevil the military; and although there had been some reforms, the attitudes of many officers and the tactics employed were still rooted deeply in the Soviet legacy. In 2013, one senior Ukrainian officer complained to the author that "even while they still paint red stars on their tanks and planes, the Russians have made so much more progress in moving past the old [Soviet-era] ways."

Reforming the military – Ground Forces

Obviously, the Russian seizure of Crimea and intervention into the Donbas provided a salutary shock. In the immediate term, the chain of command all but collapsed – not least because it was riddled with agents and sympathizers of Moscow. This crisis would galvanize an unprecedented effort to rebuild and expand the country's military capacities, and to do so in new ways – looking forward to the Western model rather than backwards to the Soviet one. Conscription was reinstated in May 2014, and a series of mobilization

Paratroopers from Ukraine's 79th Indep Air Assault Bde in 2016, riding a BTR-80 fitted with stand-off armor to defeat HEAT rounds. Note on hatch the old Soviet-style paratroop insignia, and griffin unit insignia on hull, both in white paint. (The Presidential Administration of Ukraine/Wikimedia Commons/ CC-BY-SA 4.0)

A Russian-supplied T-72B tank – note the reactive armor – captured by the Ukrainians at Debaltseve and pressed into service. Given the commonality of equipment, it is quite usual for trophies of war to be used by the other side. (Ministry of Defense of Ukraine/mil.gov.ua/ Wikimedia Commons/CC-BY-SA 4.0)

drives sought to drag reservists back into the ranks. A new generation of hungry young officers rose, replacing a sometimes hidebound old guard; money began to be spent on the Army, and the results were striking.

Overall command is the responsibility of the General Staff, reporting through the CGS to the defense minister and the president. As of 2018, the total armed forces had been built back to a strength of 182,000, half of whom were volunteers, with around 140,000 in the Ground Forces. Along with the three existing commands, in 2015 an Operational Command East was established to coordinate operations in the Donbas war (see map opposite). As of 2018 the total commitment to that conflict, across the military and the security forces, was at least 60,000 personnel.

In 2018, Kyiv stopped describing the conflict as an Anti-Terrorist Operation and instead began calling it a Joint Forces Operation. This was not mere semantics, but the acceptance of reality: that this was an open-ended military campaign, and while the Security Service of Ukraine had shaped policy when it was known as the ATO, the lead would now be taken by the General Staff.

The Ground Forces field 13 mechanized or motorized brigades, two tank brigades, two mountain warfare brigades, seven artillery brigades, and four aviation brigades. Since 2016, the Air Assault Forces have been a command in their own right, having previously been part of the Ground Forces. Like most paratroopers, they largely operate as light infantry and assault troops, with seven maneuver units: the 25th Abn Bde (Hvardiiske); 45th (Bolhrad), 46th (Poltava), 79th (Mykolaiv), 80th (Lviv) and 95th (Zhytomyr) Indep Air Assault Bdes; and the 81st Airmobile Brigade (Druzhkivka).

There is also a separate Special Forces Command, with some 4,000 operators under arms. The line units are the 3rd Special Purpose Regt at Kropyvnysky (three company-strength units); the 8th Regt at Khmelnytsky (four companies); and the 73rd Naval Special Purpose Center at Ochakiv (a three-company Naval Infantry unit). Reflecting that this is a war in which information, propaganda and psyops have been weapons as powerful as any tank, the command also has four Informational-Psychological Operations Centers: the 16th at Huiva, 72nd at Brovary, 74th at Lviv, and 83rd at Odesa.

Arms and equipment

Although Ukrainian troops now have their own camouflage clothing and insignia, a certain amount of their equipment is still Soviet legacy. Initially, Ukrainian soldiers had to rely on dated body armor – if any – or vests provided by foreign aid or private donors. New uniforms issued in 2016 went a considerable way towards providing them with modern kit, including Korsar armored vests.

Ukrainian Ground Forces/ Operational Commands, 2017. This map shows the home bases of the major units, minus those of Special Forces Command. During combat operations many are temporarily relocated.
Op Cmd West: (1) 14 Mech Bde, 39 AD Regt (Volodymir-Volinsky). **(2)** 24 Mech Bde (Yavoriv). **(3)** 80 A. Aslt Bde (Lviv). **(4)** 16 A. Av Bde (Brody). **(5)** 12 A. Av Bde (Novy Kalyniv). **(6)** 15 RA Regt (Drohobych). **(7)** 44 Art Bde (Ternopil). **(8)** 19 RA Bde (Khmelnytsky). **(9 & 10)** 128 Mtn Inf Bde (Uzhhorod & Mukachevo). **(11)** 10 Mtn Inf Bde (Kolomyla).

Op Cmd North: (12) 30 Mech Bde (Novohrad-Volynsky). **(13)** 95 A. Aslt Bde (Zhytomyr). **(14)** 28 Art Bde (Berdychiv). **(15)** 72 Mech Bde, 1128 AD Regt (Bila Tserkva). **(16)** 1 Armd Bde (Honcharivske). **(17)** 43 Art Bde (Divychky). **(18)** 59 Mech Bde (Konotop). **(19)** 27 RA Bde (Sumy). **(20)** 46 A. Aslt Bde, 18 A. Av Bde (Poltava). **(21)** 107 RA Regt (Kremenchuk).

Op Cmd South: (22) 59 Mot Bde (Haisyn). **(23)** 40 Art Bde (Pervomaysk). **(24)** 57 Mot Bde (Kropyvynytsky). **(25)** 38 AD Regt (New Odesa). **(26)** 32 Naval RA Regt (Altestove). **(27)** 28 Mech Bde (Chornomorske). **(28)** 45 A. Aslt Bde (Belhorod).

(29) 36 NI Bde, 406 Art Regt, 79 A. Aslt Bde (Mykolaiv). **(30)** 11 A. Av Bde (Chornobayivka).

Op Cmd East: (31) 92 Mech Bde (Bashkyrivka). **(32)** 25 Abn Bde, 1039 AD Regt (Hvardiiske). **(33)** 93 Mech Bde (Cherkaske). **(34)** 81 Ambl Bde (Druzhykivka). **(35)** 53 Mech Bde (Severodonetsk). **(36)** 54 Mech Bde (Bakhmut). **(37)** 17 Armd Bde (Krivy Rih). **(38)** 55 Art Bde (Zaporizhia). **(39)** 56 Mot Bde (Myrne).

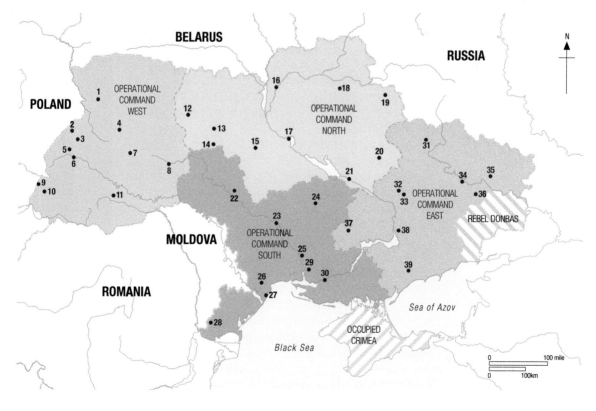

The war has created a voracious need for new recruits for the Ukrainian military. As well as multiple mobilization drives recalling reservists to arms, there is also a high-pressure campaign to attract volunteers, visible in this Kyiv street sign. (Author's Collection)

The standard personal weapons are the 5.45mm AK-74 rifle, AKS-74U assault carbine, and PM Makarov pistol, although some special forces use Ukrainian-made Fort-221 bullpup rifles and Fort-224 carbines (license-produced Israeli TAR-21s). The Fort-14TP pistol is to replace the PM when funds allow, and there are plans to replace the AK-74 with the M4-WAC47, a version of the American M4, as both an upgrade and a political statement. The SVD sniper rifle is being supplemented with locally made Zbroyar Z-10s and also Western-supplied Barrett M107A1 anti-matériel rifles. Fire support is provided by the usual array of PK and RPK-74 machine guns, along with a few Fort-101s (versions of the Israeli Negev). Soviet-vintage RPGs and other launchers will continue to dominate even as new systems are introduced, including the PSRL-1, an American-made version of the RPG-7, and the FGM-148 Javelin, the powerful American top-attack "fire-and-forget" antitank missile delivered in 2018.

Ukraine can field a small number of T-84 Oplots, but mainly still relies on the earlier T-80, along with older T-72As, and T-64s, especially locally upgraded T-64BM Bulats, with reactive armor, night sights, and a new 125mm gun. The main infantry fighting vehicle is the BMP-2, with a few upgraded BMP-1Us, while ageing MT-LB, BTR-70 and BTR-80 personnel carriers are slowly being replaced with the BTR-4. Built by the Kharkiv Morozov Machine Building Design Bureau, this can carry eight soldiers and is armed with a turreted 30mm automatic cannon, 7.62mm coaxial machine gun, and up to four antitank missiles. In addition, the Ukrainians field a wide range of light armored vehicles, including US-supplied Humvees and Soviet-vintage BRDM-2 scout cars (being upgraded to the Khazar, with new communications and sensor suites).

During the battle of Donetsk in 2014 the Ukrainians launched at least one conventionally armed SS-21 Tochka tactical ballistic missile, and many new missile, rocket and gun systems are reportedly being designed. In general, however, the Ukrainians are fielding exactly the same tube, rocket and anti-air artillery as the Russians, other than the more recent systems such as the TOS-1 thermobaric launcher.

Navy and Air Force

With a strength of 6,500, the Ukrainian Navy is really no more than a flotilla, with a single surviving Krivak III-class frigate, the flagship *Hetman Sahaydachny*; a Grisha III-class corvette, the *Vinnytsia*; a missile boat, a minesweeper, and sundry smaller and non-combat vessels. Having lost its HQ at Sevastopol (the Russians also seized the corvettes *Ternopil* and *Lutsk* when they took Crimea), it is now based out of Odesa. It regularly makes its presence known in the Black Sea, but is obviously dwarfed by the powerful Russian naval and air elements there and has played no meaningful role in

the conflict to date, beyond suffering the loss of two gunboats and a tug to the Russians in a skirmish close to the Kerch Straits in November 2018.

The clear exception are the marines of the Naval Infantry, who had suffered the same vicissitudes as the Ground Forces. In 2004 their field force, the 1st Indep Naval Inf Bde, was halved to a single battalion; although a second, the 501st Indep Naval Inf Bn, was stood up in 2013, it did not have an especially encouraging debut during the Crimean operation. Since then, however, the Naval Infantry have played a significant role in the Donbas. After a necessary period of regrouping, including adopting a new HQ at Mykolaiv, the forces of the 36th Bde, as well as the newly raised 137th Indep Naval Infantry Bn in Odesa, have been active along the line of contact. Their first casualty in the war in the Donbas was Maj Alexei Zinchenko, commanding the 73rd Naval Special Purpose Center, caught by shelling near Donetsk in August 2014.

The 36th Bde now comprises three infantry battalions (the 1st based at Mykolaiv, the 501st at Mariupol and the 503rd at Berdyansk); a tank battalion with T-80s; an artillery regiment (including an antitank battalion with the MT-12 Rapira, a rocket battalion with the BM-21, and a self-propelled gun battalion with the 2S1 Gvodzika); an engineer battalion; a reconnaissance company, a sniper company, an EW company, and other support elements. Each line battalion has one airmobile company and two regular marine companies, all mounted in BTR-80 personnel carriers. In 2018, as part of a rolling "Ukrainianization" of the military, they replaced Soviet-era insignia and swapped their black berets for blue-green ones.

The history of the independent Ukrainian Air Force has for the most part likewise been one of managing downsizing and decay; in 2014 it had retained

Elements of the Ukrainian 30th Indep Mech Bde drawn up for inspection. Note, as well as the tanks and BMPs, a mix of self-propelled guns and artillery pieces towed by MT-LB gun tractors. To the right is a 2K22 Tunguska gun/missile air defense vehicle. (Ministry of Defense of Ukraine/mil.gov.ua/ Wikimedia Commons/CC-BY-SA 4.0)

The widespread availability of surface-to-air missiles in the Donbas has severely limited Ukraine's opportunities to use its Army Aviation assets, such as this Mi-24P gunship, which can carry antitank missiles and rocket pods as well as its fuselage-mounted double-barrel 30mm GSh-30K cannon. Note the yellow-and-blue fuselage roundel. (Oleg Belyakov/AirTeamImages/ Wikimedia Commons/ CC-BY-SA 3.0)

144 of its legacy aircraft, but only two-thirds were considered airworthy. It has played a relatively small role in the war with Russia, largely because Russia has extensive AA capabilities and, if provoked, might also choose to deploy its own, much more formidable aerial assets. When Kyiv has fielded its ground-attack forces, largely Mi-24 helicopter gunships and Su-25 aircraft, this has been at considerable cost. In the first four months of the war alone they lost four Mi-24s, two Mi-8 helicopter transports, six Su-25s, three transport planes, and four strike and air-superiority jets. Several of these

Special forces operators from the Ukrainian National Guard watch as colleagues practice a rope descent from Mi-8 helicopters in 2015; note the heavy gloves to avoid friction burns. The soldier on the left has a PKM machine gun. (Ukrainian National Guard/ Wikimedia Commons/ CC-BY-SA 2.0)

While the National Guard are key combatants, they also play a substantial public security role. Here three soldiers on patrol in Kyiv in 2017 wear British-surplus DPM uniforms, and carry holstered Fort-12 pistols as well as batons. (Author's collection)

losses were from missiles fired from Russian territory. As a result, Kyiv has since been much more circumspect in its use of air assets. On the other hand, Air Command East, based at Dnipropetrovsk, has two units of long-range S-300PS surface-to-air missiles, and remains on guard in case the Russians should opt to use their airpower.

The SBU, MVS and National Guard

The Security Service of Ukraine (SBU) has played a crucial, if sometimes controversial role behind the front line in identifying Russian agents and foiling attempted sabotage. It has also gone through an extensive re-staffing, as it originally included large numbers of veterans of the old Soviet KGB and other sympathizers with Moscow. Although it claims to be totally reformed, as of 2018 many Ukrainian observers, as well as Western intelligence officials working with the SBU, regard this as still very much a work in progress. The SBU's elite counter-terrorism unit, "Alfa," was seriously hit by defections in 2014 which accounted for almost a third of its total strength. Nonetheless, it has been reconstituted, and commando teams from Alfa have played a limited but not insignificant role in the war, starting with the April 2014 siege of Slovyansk.

The Ministry of Internal Affairs (MVS) has been much more central to actual combat operations. In 2014 the MVS controlled, along with the national police force, the infamous *Berkut* riot police and the Interior Troops. *Berkut* had played such a pivotal role in the brutal attempts to suppress the 2013–14 Maidan Revolution that its survival was untenable, even had not many of its members, especially from the east of the country, deserted to

One problem for Ukraine has been the return of battle-hardened and sometimes highly motivated veterans from the volunteer battalions into the volatile world of domestic politics. These may look like riot police, but they are actually anti-government nationalist militants manning the barricades at a protest camp next to the Rada (parliament building) in Kyiv in December 2017. The sleeve patch shows they came from the Donbas Bn – see Plate G4. (Author's Collection)

the rebels. When *Berkut* was disbanded the Interior Troops – a professional, 30,000-strong paramilitary domestic security force – also naturally came under some suspicion, but were badly needed in light of the rising in the east. Consequently, they were folded into a new, expanded structure, the National Guard, also under the MVS.

A key aspect of the National Guard was that apart from inheriting the missions and personnel of the Interior Troops, it also provided a structure which could incorporate the various militias which had sprung up to fight the rebels and their Russian backers. Many of the National Guard are essentially local security personnel, tasked with backing up the police and guarding government buildings and transport hubs; for example, the 1st Important State Facilities Protection Bn guards the Chernobyl nuclear power station. However, there are also genuinely operational units; for example, the 18th Operational Regt is a motorized infantry force based in Mariupol. More common are small, sometimes specialized teams such as "Skorpion" (which protects nuclear installations), and the "Omega" and "Vega" anti-terrorist commando units. Both the last two have conducted occasional missions in the Donbas conflict, but the main role of the National Guard has been played by former militia units such as the Azov and Donbas battalions (see below).

UKRAINIAN MILITIAS

When the Donbas war started, finding the regular Ukrainian forces in complete disarray, the crisis provoked a wave of local initiatives. A range of volunteer militias arose to fight the Russians' proxies and allies, some bankrolled by powerful Ukrainian oligarchs, others rooted in local communities or political groups. Much attention has been paid to the negative aspects of this phenomenon: some were undisciplined, and others espoused nationalist views that verged on the neo-Nazi. But overall, it is undeniable that it was these fighters who stood up to the initial challenge and emerged as the first defenders of their country in those early months, when so much of the regular military was scarcely fit to fight. Over time, such groups have been incorporated to a greater or lesser extent into the forces of the Ministry of Internal Affairs – the National Guard or the Special Police Patrol Units – but many retain their own identity and even, sometimes, a degree of political and operational autonomy.

Overview: crowdsourcing national defense

The "Maidan Revolution," also known in Ukraine as the "Revolution of Dignity," had unleashed a wave of grassroots social activism. When the Russians seized Crimea and risings began in the Donbas this evolved into an upwelling of nationalism, which gave birth to a whole range of individual and local resistance efforts. The most evident were the "volunteer battalions," but they were only part of the overall process. Citizens (and supporters from abroad, especially the Ukrainian diaspora in Canada) provided soldiers and militia fighters alike with everything from body armor to medical kits, winter boots to night-vision goggles, all at their own expense. Crowdfunded initiatives even bought or built reconnaissance drones, for forces that were notably lacking in this capacity.

Against this background, it was the volunteer battalions that were crucial to the conflict ("battalions" so-called: in practice they ranged in size from unit to unit and time to time, from a large platoon all the way to a light regiment). More than 50 units were formed overall, although some proved transitory and were quickly disbanded or folded into others, even before all of them were incorporated into the National Guard or Police. Some were established by political movements and parties, typically Ukrainian nationalists. Others were essentially local militias reflecting grassroots activism or the need to resist an immediate threat. Beyond that, the Army's Territorial Defense Battalions (TDBs) were actually ad hoc units raised either by Kyiv or, more often, by local authorities.

They all tended to be light infantry, equipped with whatever small arms and support weapons they could muster, buy or steal, and were at first limited to whatever vehicles they could find in abandoned arsenals or convert from civilian trucks and cars. The AK-74 or the older AKM-47 was the standard

Soldiers from the Ukrainian Donbas Bn setting up a checkpoint in 2014; note their yellow national brassards. Recruited from locals to the area, this unit acquired a tough reputation which was reflected in its priority access to clothing and equipment, evident in the standardized uniforms and AK-74 and SVD rifles. (Lyonking/Wikimedia Commons/CC-BY-SA 4.0)

In what appears to be a photo opportunity rather than a combat situation, soldiers from the pro-Kyiv volunteer Donbas Bn disembark from their BTR-70 personnel carrier, demonstrating one of the vehicle's main flaws – that the troop compartment only has top access. (Lyonking/ Wikimedia Commons/CC-BY-SA 4.0)

personal weapon, along with a random collection of other small arms ranging from World War II-vintage bolt-action Mosin-Nagant M1891/30 rifles to imported precision rifles. Only those units bankrolled by rich business interests started with anything like a common uniform. Through 2014, many of these units developed their own funding streams – which ranged from government assistance through to, in some cases, simple looting – and began to acquire both better and more standardized equipment.

Many of these groups distinguished themselves by their tenacious willingness to fight, even when outgunned by the insurgents and their Russian backers. For example, Dnipro-1 and Right Sector volunteers were among the fabled "cyborgs" defending Donetsk Airport in 2014–15. At other times, their political agendas or their lack of discipline and training proved a serious liability. At the battle for Ilovaisk in August 2014, for example, the 500 soldiers of the 5th TDB "Prykarpattya" were charged with protecting the defenders' flank, but they broke when attacked. While some later rallied, a majority of the unit deserted, and it was subsequently disbanded. By contrast, the 700-strong Shakhtarsk Bn fought hard at Ilovaisk, but it too had to be dissolved following serious claims of looting and banditry.

Units

Some of the largest and most important retain a certain distinctiveness even after being brought into the government's security forces:

Aidar Battalion Formed by a number of figures with radical political leanings, Aidar grew to a strength of some 450 fighters by the summer of 2014; it took part in operations such as the recapture of Shchastya in Luhansk Region, but also acquired a troubling reputation for blocking humanitarian aid to civilians in the southeast, and seizing a bread factory. Its initial recognition as the 24th TDB did little to bring it under the government's control, and in 2015 it was formally dissolved, with selected members then forming a new Army unit, the 24th Indep Assault Bn "Aidar."

Azov Battalion One of the most controversial of the volunteer battalions, Azov has simultaneously a formidable reputation as a hard-fighting unit (blooded in the recapture of Mariupol in June 2014), and a questionable one for the far-right politics of many of its soldiers. Its shoulder-patch symbol recalls the *Wolfsangel*, once used by the Dutch volunteer unit of the Waffen-SS. Although formally brought into the National Guard, it has retained a strong sense of autonomy; its politics have attracted sympathizers from across Europe and beyond, as it grew first to a strength of 500 and then to a regiment. In order to placate it, as well as to reflect its high combat value, in the National Guard it has become the Special Designation Reinforced Battalion "Azov."

Batkivshchyna Battalion A force raised in Kirovohrad Region by the Resistance Movement political organization. It seems often to have been small in numbers but loud in its propaganda, not least in its optimistic claim to have destroyed the LNR's Prizrak Battalion. It became the 34th TDB.

"Chechen Battalions" While the DNR may have had the GRU-mustered Chechens of the Vostok Bn on their side, anti-Russian Chechens came to defend Ukraine. The so-called Dzhokhar Dudayev and Sheikh Mansour Bns were scarcely of company strength, and spent much time squabbling. Nevertheless, they did include both passionate fighters and also tough veterans of the Chechen Wars, with charismatic leaders such as Adam Osmayev and his surgeon-turned-sniper wife Amina Okuyeva (see Plate G3).

Donbas Battalion This force was primarily formed of fighters from the Donbas region who were loyal to Kyiv, which gave it both local knowledge and a particular passion for the conflict. It grew to more than 800 strong, and attracted instructors from the Georgian military who had fought the Russians in 2009. It eventually became part of the National Guard's 18th Operational Regiment.

Dnipro-1 Special Designation Police Patrol Regiment This force was raised by Ihor Kolomoisky, a controversial businessman and former governor of Dnipropetrovsk, who reportedly put $10 million behind it. While it played a role in the fighting, Kolomoisky appears also to have wanted to use it for his

Militiamen from the Ukrainian Azov Bn advance in an open-topped truck with improvised armor. Such makeshift personnel carriers were relatively commonplace in the early stages of the war, but proved vulnerable even to modern rifles, let alone the ubiquitous rocket and grenade launchers, and have since been replaced with military vehicles. The symbol on the side is that of the Ukrainian Patriot movement. (Carl Ridderstråle/Wikimedia Commons/CC-BY-SA 4.0)

private advantage: to ostensibly signal his commitment to the new Ukraine at a time when his business dealings were coming under adverse scrutiny, and to try to keep control of certain of his assets. Nonetheless, it was well resourced and armed, even if not particularly well trained or disciplined.

Dnipro-2 By contrast, this was a TDB of volunteers from Dnipropetrovsk, later incorporated into the regular military as its 39th Motorized Infantry Battalion.

Noman Çelebicihan Battalion Among the victims of the Russian seizure of Crimea were members of the local Tatar population, who faced immediate pressure. Crimean Tatar volunteers formed this unit in Kherson, and it would later be incorporated into Ukraine's State Border Guard Service.

OUN Battalion This force, representing the Organization of Ukrainian Nationalists, operated around Pisky. It resisted incorporation into the government's ranks, but eventually its soldiers were allowed to join the Army rather than the MVS forces.

Sich Battalion A Cossack volunteer force mustered by the nationalist Freedom Party, this never rose even to company strength. It was brought into the National Guard, becoming the 4th Co of the Kyiv Special Police Patrol Regiment.

Ukrainian Volunteer Corps This is the umbrella command for a number of units raised and initially led by Dmytro Yarosh, former leader of Right Sector (*Pravy Sektor*), an ultra-nationalist political movement. Although an early participant in the Donbas war, Right Sector's relationship with the government has always been difficult; while it cooperated with the ATO command, it did not accept its authority. Yarosh was a critic of the MVS, in particular, and this impeded attempts to incorporate Right Sector forces into the National Guard. Eventually, their 5th and 8th Bns did transfer across, but hard-liners split off to form the Ukrainian Volunteer Corps. This also claims independently still to be fielding its own "Battalion Tactical Group

G **PRO-KYIV FORCES**

(1) Militiaman, Dnipro-1 Battalion, 2014
The Dnipro-1 Special Purpose Police Bn was formed in April 2014, initially largely funded by the Ukrainian oligarch and then-governor of Dnipropetrovsk Region, Ihor Kolomoisky. As a result, it was relatively well armed and less ragtag in appearance than many comparable militia units of that time. Armed with an RPK-74, this squad machine-gunner wears battledress of the unusual Khishchnik ("predator") pattern which was used briefly by militia and MVS forces in 2014 as they scrambled to equip new units. He sports the unit's large patch of a white trident on "sky, mountains and sea," below a small blood-type tab on his right sleeve, and on his left a Ukrainian black trident on blue-and-yellow. His Army tactical vest is a Pustelya-3.

(2) Volunteer, Azov Regiment, 2015
The volunteer Azov Bn acquired an enviable reputation for its fighting spirit but a troubling one for its ultra-nationalist character, which attracted adventurers and neo-fascists from abroad. In January 2015 it was incorporated into the government's forces and became a regiment, while still retaining a strongly independent streak – thus this fighter's civilian cap and "Halloween-type" face mask. Uniform standardization has not yet reached this soldier: he wears a German Army-surplus *Flecktarn* battledress, with the left shoulder patch bearing the unit's black "wolf-hook" on yellow-and-blue. His Ukrainian Korsar M2-3 armor vest is in Dubok ("little oak") pattern, and he carries a folding-stock AKS-74.

(3) Volunteer sniper, 2014
A Chechen-Ukrainian doctor, Amina Okuyeva volunteered for the militia Kyiv-2 Battalion in 2014, and earned fame both as a battlefield medic and a sniper. Here she is cleaning rounds for her TS308 rifle, a rare licenced version of the Swiss Brugger & Thomet APR 308. This is one of a number of combinations of camouflage battledress and tactical vests in which she was photographed, always with a Muslim headscarf. Note the Ukrainian shield-and-flag patch on the slanted left sleeve pocket. As well as her sniper rifle Okuyeva carried a holstered Makarov pistol on the back of her belt for self-defense; this saved her and her husband's lives when they were attacked by an assassin posing as a journalist in June 2017. Nevertheless, her luck finally ran out that October, when she was ambushed outside Kyiv.

(4) Donbas Battalion sleeve patches
The Donbas Bn was a volunteer unit raised in 2014 by an ethnic Russian loyal to Kyiv; it was later incorporated into the National Guard as its 2nd Special Purpose Battalion. These are the unit's distinctive left-sleeve patch showing the trident as a diving eagle, and the subdued National Guard right-sleeve patch: a trident-shield on a Maltese Cross, superimposed on crossed maces.

Donbas" on the frontline, as well as 16 "reserve companies" (which are really just local party offices which also provide some paramilitary training for their members).

National Guard & Special Police Patrol units

As noted, some volunteer units, especially those which were technically TDBs, were in due course brought into the regular Army; for example, the Kryvbas TDB and the Kharkiv Bn became the 40th and 22nd Mot Inf Bns, respectively. However, most of the volunteer battalions which survived were rolled into the National Guard or the Special Police Patrol Units. Many enthusiastically welcomed the chance of official recognition and support; smaller units – such as the Svyaty Mykolai Bn (St Nicholas Bn), raised initially to defend Mykolaiv against a potential rebel attack – were quickly incorporated, but the process was not always easy.

Other units had originally been founded by charismatic individuals who enjoyed their autonomy, or had been bankrolled by oligarchs with their own interests, or reflected particular extremist political agendas. Folding these into the government forces often required careful negotiation with hard-nosed individuals. The agreement of some Right Sector fighters to transfer was only achieved following an armed stand-off at Mukachevo in western Ukraine, after fighting with local police saw at least two Right Sector fighters killed and two police cars destroyed by grenade launchers. These fighters were then given "an offer they could not refuse."

By 2017 the National Guard and Special Police were looking increasingly standardized, and while individual units had their own distinctive sleeve patches and battle-honors, the days of hand-me-down camouflage uniforms and home-made "personnel carriers" improvised from trucks covered in

Ukrainian sniper from the Azov Bn; the lettering at the bottom of his Ukrainian Patriot movement patch reads "CHYORNY/ KORPUS" ("Black Corps"). He is armed with a semi-automatic Fort 301, a rare locally produced version of the Israeli Galatz rifle. (Noah Brookes/Wikimedia Commons/ CC-BY-SA 2.0)

National Guard Main Directorate (Kyiv)
Joint Communication Center (Novi Petrivtsi)
4th Operational Bde (Hostomel)
22nd Indep Diplomatic Protection Bde (Kyiv)
NG Air Base (Oleksandriya)

1st Important State Facilities Protection Regt (Dnipro)
2nd ISFP Regt (Shostka)
4th ISFP Regt (Pavlohrad)
1st ISFP Battalion (Slavutych)
2nd ISFP Bn (Zaporizhia)
3rd ISFP Bn (Netishyn)
4th ISFP Bn (Yuzhnoukrainsk)
5th ISFP Bn (Varash)
Special Designation Detachment "Skorpion" (Kyiv)
Spec Des Detachment "Omega" (Novi Petrivtsi)

Western Operational-Territorial Command (Lviv)
2nd Indep NG Bde "Halychyna" (Lviv)
8th Operational Regt (Kalynivka)
40th Operational Regt (Vinnytska)
45th Operational Regt (Lutsk)
50th NG Regt (Ivano-Frankivsk)
13th Indep NG Bn (Khmelnitsky)
32nd Indep NG Bn (Lutsk)
4th Spec Des Bn "Kruk"
Spec Des Detachment "Vega" (Lviv)

Northern Operational-Territorial Command (Kyiv)
1st Operational Bde (Novi Petrivtsi)
4th Operational Bde (Staroye)
25th Public Security Protection Bde (Kyiv)
25th Indep NG Bn (Cherkasi)
75th Indep NG Bn (Zhytomyr)

Central Operational-Territorial Command (Dnipropetrovsk)
21st Public Order Protection Bde (Kryvyi Rih)
16th POP Regt (Dnipro)
12th Indep NG Bn (Poltava)
14th Indep NG Bn (Dnipropetrovsk)
26th Indep NG Bn (Kremenchug)

Eastern Operational-Territorial Command (Kharkiv)
3rd Operational Bde (Kharkiv)
5th Indep NG Bde "Slobozhanska" (Kharkiv)
15th Indep NG Regt (Slovyansk)
18th Operational Regt (Reinforced) (Mariupol) – incl. 2nd Spec Purpose Bn "Donbas" & Spec Des Reinforced Bn "Azov" based on those militia units
11th Indep NG Bn (Sumy)
Spec Des Intel Detachment "Ares" (Kharkiv)

Southern Operational-Territorial Command (Odesa)
23rd Public Order Protection Bde (Zaporizhia)
9th Indep Operational Rgt (Zaporizhia)
19th POP Regt (Mykolaiv)
33rd POP Regt (Odesa)
16th Indep NG Bn (Kherson)
19th Indep NG Bn (Zaporizhia)
Spec Des Detachment "Odesa" (Odesa)

Special Police Patrol Units
Regt "Dnipro-1" (Dnipropetrovsk) – based on Dnipro-1 militia
Regt "Kremenchuk" (Poltava)
Regt "Kyiv" (Kyiv) – incorporates Sich militia company
Regt "Mirotvorets" (Kyiv)
Bn "Ivano-Frankivsk" (Ivano-Frankivsk)
Bn "Kharkiv" (Kharkiv)
Bn "Kherson" (Kherson)
Bn "Luhansk-1" (Dnipropetrovsk)
Bn "Lviv" (Lviv)
Bn "Mykolaiv" (Mykolaiv) – incorporates Svyatyi Mykolai militia
Bn "Poltava" (Poltava)
Bn "Sichyeslav" (Dnipropetrovsk)
Bn "Skif" (Zaporizhiya)
Bn "Storm" (Odesa)
Bn "Suma" (Suma)
Bn "Svityaz" (Volyn)
Bn "Ternopil" (Ternopil)
Bn "Vinnitska" (Vinnitska)

steel plate were on their way out. They have their own battledress, as well as brown service dress for urban duties, reflecting their dual role as both soldiers and security personnel. While the National Guard is more directly militarized and the Special Police more often used in a law-enforcement role, in practice their duties are often interchangeable. Their equipment is essentially similar to that of the Army, with the AK-74, AKS-74U and PM as standard, albeit without some of the heavier weapons (although the National Guard does field some armored units, as well as artillery). As befits their light motorized status, they also make more use of light armored vehicles such as the locally produced KrAz Spartan.

THE FUTURE

As of the time of writing at the end of 2018, it is impossible to predict an end to the conflict. It would take a massive act of political courage for any Russian leader to surrender Crimea back to Kyiv. Although there is nothing like the same emotional and historical commitment to the Donbas, room for meaningful compromise appears limited. The tragic irony is that neither Moscow nor Kyiv really want the Donbas all that much, especially now it is war-ravaged and awash with guns, angry veterans, and virtual warlords. Yet Ukrainian President Petro Poroshenko cannot abandon Ukraine's southeast, for political reasons, any more than Russian President Vladimir Putin can admit he made a mistake in moving into it in the first place.

In 2017, Ukrainian Chief of the General Staff Gen Viktor Muzhenko suggested he could retake the Donbas in as little as ten days – albeit at the cost of 3,000 military dead and another 7,000–9,000 wounded, along with more than 10,000 civilian deaths. Whether or not he was advocating this – and there are those in Kyiv who talk of reconquering the Donbas by force some day – realistically, for the moment Moscow has "escalation dominance": there are too many ways it can surge more forces into the region or strike against Ukraine from other directions. This was especially visible in its attempts to close the Sea of Azov to Ukrainian ships in November 2018, strangling the port cities of Mariupol and Berdyansk. In 2017–18 the Ukrainians adopted tactics based on making small, incremental advances into the "gray zone" of no man's land along the line of contact, to occupy more defensible positions or ones with better fields of view, and in the process to nudge the effective border forward. However, they will hardly be able to "salami-slice" their way to victory.

That said, the expansion and reform of Ukraine's military means that the prospect of any serious further push by the Kremlin seems unlikely. They could beat the Ukrainians in a conventional war, but occupying the country would bleed Russia to death. So, for the moment, the undeclared war seems likely to continue, as an on-off conflict along the line of contact supplemented by covert Russian attempts to sabotage and subvert Ukraine. Meanwhile, Ukrainian forces are increasingly training alongside Western counterparts, and also continue to commit contingents to international missions; for instance, in 2016 a detachment from the 18th Indep Army Aviation Bde completed a tour of duty with the UN Stabilization Mission in the Democratic Republic of Congo. Such contributions are considered crucial by Kyiv, to demonstrate Ukraine's value to the international community.

H

UKRAINIAN ARMY
(1) First lieutenant, walking-out dress, 2016
This new olive-colored parade and walking-out uniform was introduced in 2016 as part of Ukraine's shift away from Soviet-legacy designs. The insignia feature Ukrainian motifs: the cap badge shows the trident on a blue cockade edged with "sunrays," set on a Maltese Cross and crossed swords; the flag is worn on the right sleeve, and a royal-blue shield patch on the left, edged yellow and bearing a yellow trident; the collar badges show a triangular foliate "tree" against crossed swords; and the trident appears on the buttons. The removable shoulder-strap slides bear the three pips of this rank, and the breast badge marks graduation from a military higher-education institute.

(2) Paratrooper, 45th Air Assault Brigade, 2018
Although the Soviet paratrooper's traditional blue-and-white *telnyashka* is retained, changes include a new maroon beret with a winged parachute-and-sword badge. Posing for journalists during a photo opportunity, he wears a pullover hooded smock and matching trousers in digital-pattern camouflage; a flag patch and the insignia of the 45th Air Aslt Bde are displayed on his left sleeve. For this public-relations occasion his Korsar M3 tactical vest is not loaded for combat.

He is showing off the new WAC-47 assault rifle, a version of the US M4 carbine manufactured by a US/ Ukrainian consortium which is being trialed to become the standard infantry weapon. It is reportedly of a modular design that allows conversion from 7.62x39mm to NATO 5.56x45mm caliber, as well as various barrel-lengths and configurations.

(3) Omega operator, 2018
"Omega" is the specialist anti-terrorism force of the National Guard, although in practice it has spent much of its time on frontline operations. This left-handed operator, cautiously checking the Kharkiv railyard after a report of possible saboteurs, wears a Kevlar Kaska-2M helmet and the unit's black coveralls, with knee-guards, gloves with padded knuckles, and superior boots. He has chosen a Perun-2 plate-carrier vest, to which he has added ammunition and equipment pouches. Omega's standard sidearm is the 9mm Fort-12 pistol, carried in a thigh drop-holster.

(4) Omega right sleeve patch
(5) Wound Medal
The war – or "Anti-Terrorist Operation," as it was termed until recently – has generated its own awards, among them this medal for Ukrainian soldiers wounded in combat.

Ukrainian President Petro Poroshenko (center) meeting commanders near the frontline. Note the digital camouflage uniforms sporting subdued patches and small flags. Poroshenko's uniform actually has a left-breast tab identifying him as "President of Ukraine," which has caused some amusement in the ranks. Behind Poroshenko is Chief of the General Staff Gen Viktor Muzhenko. (The Presidential Administration of Ukraine/ Wikimedia Commons/CC-BY-SA 4.0)

From a broader perspective, this war has provided numerous pointers to potential trends in 21st-century war. This may well prove to be the age of the deniable, full-spectrum war, widely – if inaccurately – known as "hybrid war," fought as much through disinformation, cyberattack, subversion and proxies as by direct military force. Modern wars are fought in a complex political environment, and winning the global media war is often decisive.

The Russians have demonstrated how information and communications systems are not only crucial force multipliers of the future, they are also

When it eventually ends, the war will inevitably leave a toxic legacy of mines and unexploded ordnance. Here, Ukrainian sappers gather unexploded fin-stabilized RPG and recoilless rounds in 2016. (Ministry of Defense of Ukraine/ Wikimedia Commons/CC-BY-SA 2.0)

battlegrounds. Drone-spotted artillery fires have proven lethal in shattering enemy military formations, as at Zenopillya. The Russians have also proved assiduous in jamming and spoofing not just communications but also GPS positioning signals. Beyond that, technology has also created new ways of launching psychological operations. Especially because of a lack of modern communications equipment, the Ukrainians (and many of the rebel militias) rely heavily on cellphones, which leaves them open to detection and targeting. Sometimes this is kinetic: the Russians have been tracking concentrations of phones as targets of opportunity for artillery fires. At others it is purely psychological. During the 2017 battle of Avdiivka, for example, Ukrainian soldiers began receiving text messages from unknown numbers with such uplifting sentiments as "You're like the Germans in Stalingrad" and "Your body will be found when the snow melts."

A Ukrainian soldier taking part in the multi-national exercise "Rapid Trident 2015" reloads a magazine. Note his British-surplus DPM camouflage uniform, the shield-and-flag national patch on his left sleeve, and the white recognition band tied around his right arm. The left-hand man carries an SVD sniper rifle. (Public Domain/US Army Sgt 1st Class Walter E. Van Ochten)

At the same time, this has in some ways been an intensely conventional, even traditional war. It has been a war of trenches and urban combat, of massive artillery barrages and snipers in the dawn. It has provided the West with a chance to see how the modern Russian Army has learned to fight, and the Russians a chance to test their mettle against opponents other than guerrillas. It has also reminded us that even in the age of "hybrid war," artillery remains the last argument of kings.

The various Balkan wars resulting from the collapse of Yugoslavia in 1991–92 – hitherto the only true state-to-state conflicts in Europe since the end of World War II – lasted for a decade, and left some 130,000 dead and four million displaced. It remains to be seen how long the Donbas war lasts and what its final butcher's bill will be; in the meantime, it marks a new era in European geopolitics, a new beginning for independent Ukraine, and a new challenge for Vladimir Putin's Kremlin.

SELECT BIBLIOGRAPHY

Holcomb, Franklin, *The Order of Battle of the Ukrainian Armed Forces: A Key Component in European Security* (ISW, 2016)

Howard, Colby & Ruslan Pukhov (eds), *Brothers Armed: Military Aspects of the Crisis in Ukraine,* 2nd edition (EastView, 2015)

Kofman, Michael, *"Russian Hybrid Warfare and Other Dark Arts,"* War on the Rocks, 11 March 2016 https://warontherocks.com/2016/03/russian-hybrid-warfare-and-other-dark-arts

Kofman, Michael et al., *Lessons from Russia's Operations in Crimea and Eastern Ukraine* (RAND, 2017)

Miller, James, et al., *An Invasion by Any Other Name* (IMR, 2015)

Sutyagin, Igor, *"Russian Forces in Ukraine,"* RUSI Briefing Paper, March 2015

INDEX

Page numbers in **bold** refer to illustrations and their captions.